Plays from New River *1*

Plays from New River 1

Absence by Wendy Hammond
American Girls by Hilary Bettis
Masterpiece by M.Z. Ribalow

Plays from New River series
Edited by M.Z. Ribalow

McFarland & Company, Inc., Publishers
Jefferson, North Carolina, and London

Caution: *Absence*, *American Girls*, and *Masterpiece* are fully protected under copyright laws. Professionals and amateurs are subject to a royalty for all performances. All rights, including but not limited to professional, amateur, motion picture, recitation, lecturing, public reading, radio broadcasting, television, electronic and the rights of translation into foreign languages, are strictly reserved. All rights inquiries should be addressed to Rights Department, McFarland & Company, Inc., Box 611, Jefferson, North Carolina 28640.

LIBRARY OF CONGRESS CATALOGUING-IN-PUBLICATION DATA

Plays from New River 1 / edited by M.Z. Ribalow.
    p.   cm. — (Plays from New River series)

ISBN 978-0-7864-6502-6
softcover : 50# alkaline paper ∞

1. American drama — 21st century. I. Ribalow, M. Z. (Meir Z.) II. Hammond, Wendy. Absence. III. Bettis, Hilary. American girls. IV. Ribalow, M. Z. (Meir Z.) Masterpiece.
PS634.2.P65   2011
812'.608 — dc22   2011008714

Plays from New River ISSN 2159-3094

BRITISH LIBRARY CATALOGUING DATA ARE AVAILABLE

Absence © 2011 Wendy Hammond. All rights reserved.
American Girls © 2011 Hilary Bettis. All rights reserved.
Masterpiece © 2011 M.Z. Ribalow. All rights reserved.

No part of this book may be reproduced or transmitted in any form or by any means, electronic or mechanical, including photocopying or recording, or by any information storage and retrieval system, without permission in writing from the publisher.

Front cover: The New River near "Camp New Hope" in Boggs, North Carolina (photograph by Joel Brown, 2011; JBrown@waterfrontgrp.com); comedy-tragedy theater masks and curtain background © 2011 Shutterstock

Manufactured in the United States of America

McFarland & Company, Inc., Publishers
  Box 611, Jefferson, North Carolina 28640
    www.mcfarlandpub.com

This first volume of plays in a
new series of contemporary drama is
dedicated with appreciation and love to
Dasha Shenkman,
who in so many gracious and graceful ways
has kept New River flowing.

Table of Contents

WHAT IS NEW RIVER?   1
NEW RIVER DRAMATISTS PLAY DEVELOPMENT PROCESS   7
INTRODUCTION   9

Absence by Wendy Hammond   11
American Girls by Hilary Bettis   79
Masterpiece by M.Z. Ribalow   129

ABOUT THE PLAYWRIGHTS   189
ACKNOWLEDGMENTS   191

What Is New River?

One evening in 1994 the phone rang in my Manhattan apartment. The caller identified himself as Mark Woods. He said I didn't know him, but that he had been speaking about an idea he had to Mark and Kay Ethridge, close mutual friends who lived, as he did, in Charlotte, North Carolina, and the Ethridges had immediately suggested that he call me. Woods said he wanted to schedule a phone conversation with me because, he explained, what he wished to discuss "would take some time." I said okay, and we agreed on a date to speak. Then I said: "Mark, before you hang up, why don't you give me some idea who you are and what in the world you're calling about." Four hours later, we were still talking passionately, and three things were already clear. First, we were kindred spirits. Second, that though we shared the same unusual ambition — establishing a creative Eden where talented writers could be nurtured and encouraged to raise the level of their storytelling to even greater heights — we were coming at it from very different yet complementary directions. He wanted to build it and I wanted to run it. And third, the Ethridges were right: Woods and I were a serendipitous professional match.

It took almost five years for Mark to find the perfect location for what we were then calling The Playwrights Project. It was at Healing Springs, in Ashe County, North Carolina, in the woods of the Blue Ridge Mountains, on the banks of the New River. Eventually, in honor of the river flowing past us and the new stream of creativity flowing from our writers, we re-named ourselves New River Dramatists.

Our first week, in March 1999, was unforgettable. We held our sessions in an abandoned schoolhouse which its owner allowed us to occupy both for that week and for the eight summers that followed. We stayed at River House, a jewel of a country inn two miles down the road, owned and run by Gayle Winston, a wonderful, wildly supportive angel (and famed chef, to boot) whom we soon referred to as the Goddess of Grassy Creek (where River House was officially located).

While Mark spent every waking hour trying to garner support for our endeavor, I established a structure for the work itself. We had a dozen seats at the table (both by artistic preference and financial limitations) and I invited four writers and eight actors to participate in reading, critiquing and developing the writers' work (as time passed, that evolved into five writers and seven actors, allowing some flexibility in those cases where an artist was both). The writers had mornings and nights to write. After lunch, we would all gather to read and discuss plays for four to six hours five to six afternoons a week.

Our process is much unchanged to this day (the table rules follow this piece). I'd been confident it would work, because much of my life — creating literary departments and theatre companies, and as a professional reader and writer of plays and screenplays — had been an unwitting preparation for just such an enterprise.

But when we gathered that first week in March 1999, my confidence in this process was unsupported by hard evidence. Ten years later, when we gathered for another week in March 2009, this time at River House itself, to commemorate and celebrate our first ten years, the resulting statistics were difficult to argue with. We had supported the work of some 70 playwrights who in turn had developed some 345 plays and screenplays, close to half of which had been either produced or optioned. Their work had been presented at major theatres around the world, and our writers had been awarded a cornucopia of literary prizes, including the National Book Award, the Simonovitch Prize, the August Wilson Award, and the National Medal of the Arts.

The key to our process is that New River does not produce. Ever. (We don't encumber, either.) This means all our attention is on encouraging the development of the work, not getting it ready for public display next Tuesday. We don't care if a writer works on a different project every time he brings one in, or changes her mind just before the session. We don't care if they finish a piece, or start three new ones. We're not producing plays; we're nurturing gifted writers so that their work, already fine, may be better than it would otherwise have been. Mark and I agreed early on that we wanted to pay each of the artists $500 per week, in addition to room, board and transportation, because it was so important to make pellucid our respect for their talents.

At New River, comments must address what the writer is trying to write, not what anyone else thinks he or she *should* write. Our first summer, Cassandra Medley, a terrific writer who happens to be an African-American woman, was writing a play about a "lily" (a black woman so light-skinned she passes easily as white) in 1957 Detroit. Zena is married to Brian, a white auto executive who has no idea she is other than a southern belle. Cassandra would bring in two or three scenes every other day, and the comments would raise questions that helped her continue to write it the way she wanted to. At the end of the first week, she had the entire first act, so we read it all to see how it sounded so far.

We ask writers to be silent during the initial round of comments, so as to quell potential defensiveness and have them listen instead to what everyone thought they heard. I refrained from commenting; the moderator has a greater value listening to what everyone else has to say, then synthesizing the major points that seem to keep occurring before inviting direct questions as well as further comments, during which time the writer can say whatever she (or he) wants.

When the first wave of comments was completed, I said to Cassandra: "I've heard eight comments which superficially sounded as if they were about different points, but they're really all tributaries of the same stream. And that stream is an uncertainty on the part of the audience as to how much she does or doesn't love Brian."

She interrupted me with, "No, she does love him, she really does."

To which I said, "If she loves him, that's fine with me; it's your play. If she doesn't love him, that's also fine with me; it's your play. But that's eight people that don't know one way or the other. There are only twelve of us in the room, and two of the remaining four are you and me. So whatever Zena feels about him, it isn't clear, is it, Cass?"

While she laughed, I continued, "And if you do want her to love him — since that's what you just said — you need to bring him into the play, because he clearly isn't there yet. *We* don't have to love him; we just need to believe that *she* does."

By the time she had completed the play, Cassandra had the entire room caring about Brian. And by developing Brian she also strengthened Zena, because now it *mattered* whether she stayed with him or not.

As crucial as we feel it is to help writers question, clarify and improve their work, we regard it as equally critical to encourage writers to write not what they are told might be most saleable, but what they know in their souls will be most true to their gifts: to write not for Caesar, but rather for God and the Unknown Friend.

James McLure, an experienced and much-lauded playwright, was working one summer on a two-character piece that seemed to me clearly an attempt to write something slick rather than from the *kishkes*. One night I asked him: was this the play he truly wanted, in his heart of hearts, to write? If so, I assured him, he would have our total support. But I wondered if he had really come to our mountain retreat to write this.

Well, no, he admitted. But there was really no point in writing the play he really wanted to write.

Why not? I asked.

Because, he said, there were 24 characters in it, and no one would ever produce it.

Good, I said. Write that one.

Really?

Sure. If you don't write it here, you never will. And if you do write it here, you'll be able to hear it. We can double or triple roles if need be, and we cast without regard to gender, age or race anyway.

But no one will produce it, he repeated, so what was the point?

Look at it this way. If you write the two-hander, in all likelihood no one will produce that one either, right?

He agreed wryly.

So no matter what you write, no one will do it anyway. So why not write the play your heart is in? That way, when they reject it, at least they'll be turning down what you really wanted to say.

That made sense to him, and he decided to write the large, intense piece that became *Blue Silence*, about a universe of good (not to be confused with honest) cops. The room had a great time developing it, because of its heartfelt passion and intelligence. Ironically, of the forty plays to emerge from New River that summer, *Blue Silence* became the first to be fully produced (in Los Angeles).

So that's our mission: to find the best writers we can and relentlessly encourage them to write whatever is truest and most important to them. Of course, to do this means constructing a creative community with considerable thought and care. If we have five writers and seven actors, we make sure the writers (as well as the actors) have a certain diversity: women and men, veterans and new writers, different backgrounds, ethnicities — as much of a balance as we can manage while making sure each writer is someone in whose talent we passionately believe.

With actors, we search for an unusual combination of characteristics. When you're casting a production of a play in New York, you go for the best actor available, and don't worry whether they go home at night and perform odd religious rituals while speaking in tongues. But in a community like New River where everyone is basically living together while working on an extraordinary variety of writing styles and subjects, the demands are different. Outstanding talent is of course a *sine qua non*, but we also need actors of extraordinary range, for they have to read an exceptionally wide variety of roles. They must possess keen intelligence, so that they can make helpful comments in a supportive fashion; be articulate enough to express their thoughts with cogent incisiveness; and be ensemble-minded enough to leave their egos at home.

The success of New River is based on how much the writers and actors inspire each other (we change some participants each week, so that no two weeks are ever exactly the same mix of artists). Many writers have remarked on how helpful this process has been. Jack Heifner, playwright of *Vanities*, calls our process "probably the most positive feedback I've had of my work in the 25 years I've been writing in the theater." Sharon Pomerantz, now known for her novel *Rich Boy*, says, "We felt lifted to a place of honor, as if the very fabric of society depended on what we were doing … and it does." Denis Johnson, who subsequently won the National Book Award for *Tree of Smoke*, tells us, "I learned lessons I'll always treasure — the experience changed me." And Pulitzer laureate N. Scott Momaday simply says, "If I could spend a month in a place like this, I could write something REALLY good."

Now you know what some of the playwrights think of New River. But don't take their word — or ours. Read these three plays. See for yourself.

M.Z. Ribalow • Artistic Director • New River Dramatists

New River Dramatists Play Development Process

Table Rules

Read the play (or scenes). The first time should be a cold reading, so that people can comment on what they thought it was before they actually knew. Since only the introductory reading of the work can be cold, take advantage of that fact.

Cast the roles at the table. Whenever possible, use different actors from act to act, or even scene to scene. That way, the writer hears different voices; even when they are not the ideal ones, there are lessons to be learned from listening to different takes on the same character. In addition, the actors become more collegial and less competitive; there is no reason for them to compete when no one is being cast.

Discussion Rules

Discussion begins with the moderator soliciting comments from those around the table. Only the invited participants of the group should comment; outside observers are asked to simply observe. When someone wishes to speak, they raise their hand or otherwise signal for recognition, but they do not interrupt out of turn, which would lead to outspoken members dominating the comments and more reserved artists rarely being able to share their observations.

The first round of observations consists of comments only. Direct questions should wait until the next stage of discussion. During these initial comments, the writer should not respond to any critique. This will prevent the writer from becoming quickly defensive, and require him or her to listen to what everyone thought the play was and wasn't doing, whether that matched the written intention or not. Such realizations can be quite useful.

After the first wave of comments have been heard, the moderator will summarize and synthesize the major points that keep recurring in people's perspectives, as well as add other observations that have not yet been made. The moderator's remarks will function as a bridge to the next stage, which will be further comments or direct questions. At this point, the writer should feel free to respond to anything at all.

At all times, participants should express agreement or disagreement with any comment by employing a thumbs up or down gesture rather than by repeating or rephrasing the observation. The moderator will take note of thumbs when such displays warrant notice.

Discussion will continue until the writer has had all his or her questions addressed.

During the discussion, there are four rules that shall be observed and will, if necessary, be enforced. They are as follows:

(1) All comments must be constructive. No trashing is allowed, ever. Comments such as "I hate these people, I wish they'd die" help no one. It is far more useful to note that an audience might feel more involved if given more reason to care about these characters and what happens to them.

(2) All comments must address the play being written, not the one you would have written (even if you are convinced yours might have been better). Everyone is there to help the writer write the play *that writer* aspires to write. If the play is about cowboys, it is irrelevant that it does no justice to the Apache. Nor does it matter whether it is radical or revolutionary or reactionary; what matters is whether whatever pattern it is trying to establish requires more yellow in the corner.

(3) No invidious comparisons are allowed. It is unhelpful to say that Shakespeare did this better or that Jane Austen's work has a more mature perspective on the issue. Limit comments to the work at hand.

(4) No one, ever, is allowed to tell a writer how to rewrite. They know how to rewrite, and why they may choose not to. Wonder aloud whether knowing more about a character's motivation might be helpful to this story; do *not* say "what you need is a scene in which Mark enters the room, shoots six people and then drinks some lemonade."

Within these parameters, comments are welcomed.

Introduction

This is the first volume of *Plays from New River*, showcasing a place where gifted writers of plays and screenplays are paid and nurtured to write whatever they most want to write. These three very different plays are among the results. *Absence* considers an era of American foreign policy by focusing on the intensely human story of a Mormon couple caught in the collateral damage of those times. *American Girls* shows us the hilariously terrifying results when teenage girls grow up in a culture that simultaneously worships Christianity and celebrity. *Masterpiece* raises timeless questions about the nature of art, the relation of reality to illusion, when lies become truth, and who gets to decide these dilemmas. Each play has a distinctive voice, subject and style. What they share in common is that they were all developed at New River, though at different sessions: *Absence* when we began, around 2000; *Masterpiece* around 2006; and *American Girls* more recently, in 2008.

Absence was first fully produced by People's Light and Theatre Company, opening on October 16, 2009. *The Broad Street Review* wrote that "Wendy Hammond's powerful *Absence* ... incisively develops her characters and makes plausible the tremendous life changes they undergo." This remarkable play, searingly honest in its examination of how a career that corrupts the spirit can also poison a marriage, awaits further productions.

American Girls was produced at New York City's 45th Street Theatre in 2008, with the playwright acting (opposite Kira Sternbach) in her own play. Her burgeoning talent was rapidly recognized. *New York Cool* wrote that "a surprising and original new voice is making its debut" and that "American girls — and boys — haven't heard the last from this impressive young writer."

Masterpiece was first staged at the Armour Street Theatre in Davidson, North Carolina, in February 2011, after outstanding readings in New York City, where Jon Sobel at blogcritics.org wrote: "Erudite and suspenseful.... The script deals easily with complex matters of philosophy and culture: what is authenticity? What is genius and what mere craft? What is the role of the critic? There are no villains or heroes in Ribalow's telling ... its characters touch our hearts as powerfully as its language tickles the brain," and Laura Shaine Cunningham, author of *Sleeping Arrangements* and *A Place in the Country*, wrote: "It is rare to find a play so intelligent and entertaining and also informative.... I was at the edge of my seat as the true life plot twists unfolded and the playwright's wit hit every target. This play has a great future and deserves a permanent place in the literature of theater."

Absence
by Wendy Hammond

Absence was first produced by People's Light and Theatre Company, opening on October 16, 2009.

ARTISTIC DIRECTOR: Abigail Adams
MANAGING DIRECTOR: Grace E. Grillet
DIRECTOR: Ken Marini
SET DESIGNER: Arthur R. Rotch
LIGHTING DESIGNER: Gregory Scott Miller
PRODUCTION STAGE MANAGER: Patricia G. Sabato
PRODUCTION MANAGER/SOUND DESIGNER: Charles T. Brastow
COSTUME DESIGNER: Lisa Zinni
DRAMATURG: Elizabeth Pool
FIGHT DIRECTOR: Samantha Bellomo

Cast
PETER—Greg Wood
MARY—Judith Lightfoot Clarke

Absence grew out of another Hammond play, *The Hole*, which was developed and performed at The Purple Rose Theatre. *Absence* was developed by New River Dramatists. Thanks especially to Jeff Daniels, Murphy Davis, Seth Gordon, Randell Haynes, Susan Knight, Ken Marks, Michael Medeiros, Patricia Randell, Victor Slezak, Guy Sanville, and Mark Woods.

I dedicate the play, with much gratitude, to Meir Ribalow.

SET: A room, simple and stark. Sepia tones. Tilted perspective. A door stage left and a door stage right. Stage left door has a chain lock on it. News clips are projected onto the back wall between scenes. Upstage a scrim on which cuts from newsreels will be projected. Newsreel cuts are short and will overlap. They can become surreal at times.

CHARACTERS: Peter and Mary

ACT I
Scene One
A Student Garret, Cambridge, Massachusetts, April 1945

(Newsreels of the war in Germany. Lights up on a table and two chairs, books, papers and clothes strewn all over. Peter comes on with a bucket and mop. He considers a moment how to mop a floor. He's never done this before. He sticks the mop in the bucket and then puts it on the floor. But he didn't squeeze the mop so the floor now has a little lake of water on it. He considers the lake. He steps in it. Small splash. He jumps in it. Splash! He smiles. He jumps in it several more times. Splash! Splash! Splash! Knocking)

PETER. Mary?

MARY. *(from off, muffled)* Yes?

PETER. You're early.

MARY. *(from off)* Yes. *(He looks around the room at the mess. A look of horror comes into his face. Then he leaps into action swiping up the lake with the washcloth, it doesn't work, he grabs a shirt off a pile of laundry and tries to soak up the lake. Finally he grabs several other shirts and lays them over the lake. More knocking)*

MARY. *(from off)* Peter?

PETER. Just a minute. *(He runs to the table and pushes off the stacks of books and papers, looks with horror at the dirt on the tabletop. He grabs a frayed quilt off a chair and throws it over the table like a tablecloth. Insistent knocking)*

MARY. *(from off)* Peter?

PETER. Just a minute! *(He lifts the quilt and shoves the stack of books under the table. He shoves the mop and bucket under the table. The handle of the mop sticks out. He pushes it in but then the head of the mop sticks out. He pushes the head of the mop in but then the handle sticks out. Pounding)*

MARY. *(from off)* You all right? Peter?

PETER. In a minute! *(He throws the shirt over the sticking out mop handle. He grabs a glass with a daisy in it and plunks it down on the table. He runs to the door and opens it)*

PETER. I'm sorry, I was... Come in. Please. Please come in. *(Slowly, tentatively, Mary steps in. She carries a suitcase. She looks all around. She is frightened. Peter takes the suitcase from her but he's not sure where to put it. Then he sets it down where he's standing. He looks up and catches her eye. They both look immediately away. He laughs. She laughs)*

MARY. Did you hear?

PETER. What?

MARY. The Germans are about to surrender.

PETER. I heard.

MARY. Any moment now. Can you feel it? The air is full of light. *(She looks up and catches his eye. They both immediately look away. She laughs. He laughs)*

PETER. Oh. Sorry. I'm sorry. *(He takes a pile of laundry off a chair and holds it out for her to sit. Tentatively, she sits)*

MARY. What's that smell?

PETER. Wha — Oh. I was cooking.

MARY. Oh.

PETER. I was cooking you a stew. I figured you'd be hungry.

MARY. Yes.

PETER. It didn't work out.

MARY. I'm sorry.

PETER. I'm a terrible cook.

MARY. Well your mother never taught you.

PETER. But you. You're a very good cook.

MARY. My mother taught me.

PETER. Would you like some milk? I'll get you some milk.

MARY. Thank you.

PETER. It's better than nothing. Milk. Oh no.

MARY. What?

PETER. Out of milk.

MARY. Oh.

PETER. Let's see. There's an onion. Sardines!

MARY. No thank you.

PETER. But you must be starving.

MARY. Really, I'm fine.

PETER. I'd go buy you food but I'm completely out of cash. I've got plenty of coupons.

MARY. Are we the only ones here?

PETER. My roommate's here. Well not right now. He'll be here as soon as the library closes.

MARY. When will that be?

PETER. Soon. You think I'll...? I would never... You're not that kind of... I respect you, I do, I respect you very much!

MARY. *(stands)* I should go.

PETER. But you came all this way!

MARY. But we're alone. I better go. *(starts to leave)*

PETER. *(suddenly)* We could go have a soda! There's a shop just downstairs!

MARY. But you're completely out of cash.

PETER. *(deflates)* That's right. *(an idea)* What if we…?

MARY. What?

PETER. I don't know if you'll like this.

MARY. Why?

PETER. What if we… well… prayed together. Because if we ask for Jesus' presence to be with us we're not alone, problem solved. *(humiliated)* I thought you wouldn't like it.

MARY. I think it's a wonderful idea.

PETER. You do?

MARY. Wonderful. *(She folds her arms and bows her head. He clasps his hands, closes his eyes and opens his mouth. But he can't bring himself to say the prayer)*

PETER. We could say a silent prayer!

MARY. Yes. *(They bow their heads and pray silently. Peter peeks at Mary. She's praying intensely. Finally—)*

MARY. Peter?

PETER. What?

MARY. Do you feel him?

PETER. *(devastated)* I'm sorry. I —

MARY. I do.

PETER. Really?

MARY. I feel him.

PETER. As long as one of us does.

MARY. Yes! *(He smiles. She sits. He sits)*

PETER. Thank you for coming. Thank you. You don't know what this means to… Especially since you've never… I don't think you've ever… Have you ever been outside Utah before?

MARY. No.

PETER. Thank you… Because it's… Because I have something to ask you.

MARY. You said.

PETER. I did?

MARY. In the letter.

PETER. Did I say what it was?

MARY. No.

PETER. Oh.

MARY. So?

PETER. Excuse me?

MARY. What is it?

PETER. What?

MARY. What you have to ask me?

PETER. *(beat, then blurting)* We could talk first, couldn't we? It's not as if there are guns pointed at our heads. There isn't a bomb about to go off!

MARY. *(baffled)* What do you want to talk about?

PETER. I don't know. What do you want to talk about?

MARY. I don't know.

PETER. Well you better think of something. We can't just sit here gawking at each other, nothing to say.

MARY. You're the one who wanted to talk.

PETER. But I'm no good at it! You're good at it! At Church, you always had a crowd around you, hanging on every word, enrapt. Me, I never got anyone to listen to more than a sentence.

MARY. Maybe if they weren't so long.

PETER. Long?

MARY. I didn't mean it like —

PETER. *(very upset)* I'm *long? Longwinded?*

MARY. No. No…

PETER. I'm sorry. I'm overreacting. It's just… well I've never been in this situation! I haven't the slightest idea how to behave!

MARY. Me either.

PETER. You don't?

MARY. No.

PETER. Are you… a little… maybe…

MARY. What?

PETER. Nervous?

MARY. Yes. Oh.

PETER. I'm so relieved.

MARY. Very nervous. Very very nervous!

PETER. Thank God! *(They look up at each other. They laugh)*

MARY. I know. Why don't we be quiet for a minute. Just sit here quietly. Eventually a subject will have to occur to one of us.

PETER. All right. *(Silence. They glance at each other hoping the other has something to say)*

MARY. *(finally)* I could tell you about home!

PETER. Yes! Home!

MARY. There's the war effort. I help collect rubber tires.

PETER. Good for you.

MARY. Bishop Phelps holds prayer meetings Tuesdays for the boys who are fighting. I try to pray myself several times a day, but it always makes me think of…

PETER. What?

MARY. *(upset)* Nothing. I mean…

PETER. What?

MARY. Tell me about here. What's it like here? I never knew anyone who went to any graduate school much less Harvard Graduate School of Political Science.

PETER. Well. I study... well... a lot.

MARY. And the people here? Are they different?

PETER. Very different.

MARY. How?

PETER. They're... Well everything is... In every way... Every face I see is unfamiliar. Every person I speak to is some other strange religion. Even the way they walk here! As if they're fighting the concrete! People walk gently in Utah. I can't tell you how much I miss people walking gently!

MARY. Oh Peter.

PETER. And then there's...

MARY. What?

PETER. Well it's... I mean it's not the sort of thing you say... out loud.

MARY. Why not?

PETER. I don't even like to tell myself. If it comes into my mind I open a book and study like mad. Or write a paper even if the paper hasn't been assigned. I suppose that's why I get As in every class.

MARY. At least there's a benefit.

PETER. And if that doesn't work, I pretend it's happening to someone else. A professor of mine. We call him Dr. H. I have to admit I don't like Dr. H. And for some reason I can't figure out he's touted as a genius, the mind who will lead us into the next era of political evolution! Perhaps I'm jealous. He's not quite two years older than I am and already he's a tenured professor. Of course I'm jealous! I'll try to pray more about it. As it is now, I pray every morning, and then every afternoon I step into his class with those bulging eyes bulging even more behind those thick, black framed glasses. He looks like a sea monster! And I don't know why he's chosen me in particular, my desk particularly, but whenever he wants to make a point he leans over my desk, his black frames hovering right next to my face... And then!

MARY. What?

PETER. He spits!

MARY. Oh my!

PETER. "OB JEC TIVE!" That's his favorite word. "OB JEC TIVE!" He has a thick foreign accent. *(German accent)* "We must remain OB JEC TIVE!" Every so often I take out my handkerchief and wipe my face but he doesn't take the hint! *(Peter stops suddenly. He is confused)* I didn't mean to talk about that. I meant to talk about something else...

MARY. *(prompting him)* Something happens to you.

PETER. Hm?

MARY. And you pretend it happens to Dr. H.

PETER. Do you think that's unchristian of me? We all have our quirks. Who am I to judge? Me? I'm longwinded. Boring!

MARY. No.

PETER. Yes. To be objective, I'm tedious. It's better to face it. And him. Dr. H. Once you get past his physical attributes — and that curly *greasy* hair... For example he can talk about Russia or Syria or Japan for hours and you're... Once he invited some of us to dinner. His girlfriend cooked. Well one of his girlfriends. Imagine looking like that and still he has a whole pack of girlfriends! But that isn't my point. The point is we're at dinner and he starts a spontaneous lecture on India's civil unrest. He doesn't finish his subject 'til three in the morning! Not for one *moment* does my mind wander. He is... riveting.

MARY. So you do like him.

PETER. Yes. What I meant was... What I don't like... I almost yelled at him yesterday... I almost shouted. I... *(he thinks)* Dr. H, the way he talks about war, foreign policy, even what he says about his girlfriends, it's all so devoid of... As if all human interactions are nothing more to him than... For instance, if Dr. H were here right now in this room, he would see nothing more than two human objects he could manipulate to his advantage. Like pawns in a chess game. He would completely miss we are Mary and Peter who are... perhaps... *(very difficult to say)* falling in... love... He would miss that. *(She flushes, nonplussed. He is horrifically humiliated)* I shouldn't have said that.

MARY. No. You... I mean —

PETER. That was presumptuous, premature. Let's pretend I didn't say that!

MARY. No, Peter —

PETER. *(abruptly running over her)* Have you read any Metternich?

MARY. No.

PETER. Dr. H obsesses over him lately. I'd be interested to know what you thought. *(awkward pause)*

MARY. Did you hear about Harlan and Fran? They're getting married.

PETER. I thought they didn't like each other.

MARY. They do now. They're getting married next Wednesday.

PETER. She used to say he was phony. And he called her Sister Block of Ice.

MARY. I told them about your letter and Harlan said congratulations but I said I wasn't sure what you want to ask me. Not 'til you actually ask me. Perhaps you ought to ask me now and get it over with. I'm on pins and needles...! Peter?

PETER. Mm?

MARY. Did you hear what I said?

PETER. What was that?

MARY. *(crushed)* Nothing. Never mind. *(awkward pause)*

PETER. I think I'll ask you now.

MARY. *(perks up)* Really?

PETER. I was wondering if... What I mean is... Of all the girls I grew up with... And we had a good time, don't you think?

MARY. Lovely.

PETER. How we sat on the grass eating pears?

MARY. You dripped on your tie.

PETER. You're not engaged to anyone else, are you?

MARY. No.

PETER. Will you…? I mean… do you…? I mean I never planned to marry, Mary. In fact I always planned not to. Marriage always seems to make people miserable. My parents… Do you know one married couple who are happy?

MARY. How could they be? There's been the Depression and then the war.

PETER. But marriage should fix all that, don't you think? At least it should provide comfort. But from what I've seen marriage makes the harshness of life even harsher. Take your parents for instance. Your father's always snapping at your mother.

MARY. Snapping?

PETER. Yes! And your mother's gotten fat!

MARY. How can you say that, Peter?!

PETER. The same thing will probably happen to you. I think it's started already. Your face looks fuller.

MARY. Really?

PETER. I think you've gained ten pounds since the last time I saw you. Oh my God.

MARY. What…? *What?*

PETER. It's happening.

MARY. What's happening?

PETER. What I pretend happens to Dr. H but it doesn't happen to Dr. H, it happens to me. It's happening right now. A part of me is… disappearing!

MARY. What part?

PETER. Obviously this isn't real. It's all in my mind. But I can't seem to get rid of it. I walk down the street on my way to Church or class, people whizzing by me on the sidewalk, and I feel myself… evaporate. Here… *(touches his chest)* As if there's a hole. As if I could look in a mirror and see all the way through to the wall behind me.

MARY. Is it painful?

PETER. Worse! Disappearing is worse!

MARY. When did this start?

PETER. Let's not talk about that.

MARY. Why?

PETER. *(testy)* Because let's not.

MARY. Why did you ask me to come all this way if you're not willing to be open with me?

PETER. *(lashing out)* We can't be open about everything! We've got to keep some things to ourselves!

MARY. I don't agree with that at all.

PETER. You're the only person I've ever told. Why can't you be grateful for that?! *(Furious, Mary turns away from him. Peter realizes he just made a mistake)*

MARY. Jesus is here?

PETER. Yes.

MARY. How do you know?

PETER. I… feel him.

MARY. You're not just saying that to keep me here?

PETER. No.

MARY. I'm not sure you're telling me the truth. Maybe you don't even believe in Jesus anymore.

PETER. Of course I believe in —

MARY. Mother says you would have lost your faith.

PETER. Why would I do that?

MARY. She says everyone who moves out of Utah loses their faith.

PETER. Who else ever moved out of Utah?

MARY. Mother had two friends growing up who moved to Ohio. They became Christian Scientists.

PETER. What about the boys who went off to the war? Does she think they'll lose their faith too?

MARY. No, because they'll come back. Hopefully. *(Mary's lip begins to quiver)*

PETER. Your brother. I'm sorry. Is it very hard on your mother?

MARY. What do you think?

PETER. I think it must be very hard.

MARY. He was going to be a schoolteacher.

PETER. I'm… sorry. *(She puts her hand over her face trying to control herself. Awkwardly, Peter strokes her hair. He's never done something like this before)*

PETER. I didn't mean to call you fat. You're not fat. I don't know what comes over me.

MARY. I can't feel Jesus anymore.

PETER. He's sitting on the chair.

MARY. Peter.

PETER. No, on the counter.

MARY. Come on.

PETER. Yes. Cross-legged.

MARY. No!

PETER. Yes!

MARY. Cross-legged! *(They laugh. They stop laughing)* I think about what you said.

PETER. When?

MARY. On the grass. I think about it every day.

PETER. *(horrified)* Oh. I'm sorry.

MARY. Why?

PETER. I sounded sound so… well… pedantic. Ridiculous.

MARY. No. It was… beautiful.

PETER. Really?

MARY. *Beautiful.*

PETER. I think I'll ask you now.

MARY. Please do.

PETER. I think I'm ready. *(kneels in from of her)* Will you…? Do you believe in destiny?

MARY. Well. I don't know.

PETER. *(stands)* Either you do or you don't, Mary. Which?

MARY. I don't think it's up to me to decide such a thing.

PETER. So that's your answer. You don't know.

MARY. I don't know and I don't care to know. Peter, I wish you'd hurry up and ask the question you referred to in your letter. I'm so tired my eyes feel full of sandpaper.

PETER. That *was* the question.

MARY. What was?

PETER. What I just asked.

MARY. Do I believe in destiny.

PETER. Yes.

MARY. You had me cross the whole country for do I believe in destiny?!

PETER. Not the whole country.

MARY. Almost the whole country!

PETER. It's a very important question.

MARY. You couldn't have asked your roommate?!

PETER. He wouldn't have understood.

MARY. I'm afraid I don't either!

PETER. You've got to try, Mary.

MARY. Peter. I've just been on a train for four days and nights, third class, the food my mother packed me ran out in Chicago, and since Columbus a fat man has been sitting next to me smoking the most revolting cigars! I thought you would ask me to marry you! What an idiot I am! I would have said yes! Stupid idiot! Do you realize I turned down seven other proposals! Seven! But I would have said yes to you!

PETER. Why, Mary?

MARY. I don't know! It doesn't make sense! We had one date! I always thought I'd marry a businessman like George. He'll be the president of ZCMI someday and when he proposed to me I meant to say yes but instead out of my mouth came no! I said it so loud it echoed in the church auditorium — no no no no no no.

PETER. But you would have said yes to me?

MARY. I don't know why. Mother says you give her the creeps! Once, you were 12 years old, you gave a talk in Sunday school titled, "Brigham Young, Creator of the Only True Communist Society." Sister Horst almost choked to death. That same year, during the Christmas party, I found you behind the coat rack reading *The Politics and Economics of the Middle East*! Where did you find such a book?

PETER. You have no idea why you would have said yes?

MARY. None whatsoever!

PETER. You see? Destiny!

MARY. What on earth are you talking about?!

PETER. Please sit down, Mary. I can't explain anything with you flying around like this.

MARY. *(grabs her suitcase)* I can't sit down! I have to go back to the train station! *(He stands in front of the door)*

PETER. You can't go. I won't let you.

MARY. Now you're going to ruin me on top of everything else? Mother said this would happen.

PETER. Mary, you haven't eaten for two days. If you go now you'll faint on the street.

MARY. You're right. *(She collapses in a chair)*

PETER. I don't want to ruin you, Mary. I just want you to eat some sardines. *(Rushes off to get the sardines)*

MARY. But then I'm going.

PETER. *(from off)* Maybe you'll change your mind by then.

MARY. *(jumps up)* I'm going.

PETER. *(runs on)* No! Please! Just eat some sardines first! I promise you can go after you eat some sardines! *(She collapses again. He hands her the open can of sardines and a fork)*

MARY. No plate?

PETER. Sorry. *(She rolls her eyes, but then dives in eating)* You see… What I mean is… I mean my point…

MARY. You'd better hurry. I've eaten three of these already.

PETER. It's just… what I'm about to…

MARY. Four.

PETER. I don't want to shock you.

MARY. Five!

PETER. All right, all right. My father. When I was four he came home one night. Emma, he said. He was hanging up his coat. I lost my job, Emma.

MARY. Everybody did. It was the Depression.

PETER. Sometime after that my father went away, remember? He got work in Wyoming? But he didn't really get work in Wyoming. That's just what we told everyone at Church.

MARY. He got put away in the loony bin.

PETER. You know?!

MARY. Everyone knows.

PETER. Everyone?!

MARY. Why do you think people were always bringing you dinners? Leaving hand me down clothes at your back door?

PETER. From the *beginning*?! Everyone knew from the *beginning*?!

MARY. Peter. Your father stood on park benches naked shouting Shakespeare speeches.

PETER. *People knew that?!*

MARY. How could we miss it, Peter?

PETER. OFFICER JENSEN SAID NOBODY SAW!

MARY. It only takes a couple people seeing something like that and it spreads through the whole state.

PETER. *THE WHOLE STATE!*

MARY. I didn't mean literally the whole state. I'm sure there are several people in Utah who don't know.

PETER. PEOPLE HAVE BEEN LAUGHING AT ME? MY WHOLE LIFE PEOPLE HAVE BEEN *SNIGGERING BEHIND THEIR HANDS?!*

MARY. I'm sure they're haven't been sniggering.

PETER. *I'm sure they HAVE!* (Peter slams himself down in the chair and puts his head in his hands)

MARY. Peter. I'm sorry. I shouldn't have told you but I'm just so tired and hungry, and imagine how upended I felt when the question you asked me wasn't what I had in mind at all! Not at all! *(Peter doesn't move)* I don't think they're sniggering, Peter. People are kinder than that. *(He still doesn't move. Mary picks up her suitcase)* Mother will be angry with me when I tell her what happened. She'll be full of I-told-you-so's. *(She starts to leave)*

PETER. Mary? It stopped.

MARY. What stopped?

PETER. The hole. It stops when I'm...

MARY. What?

PETER. Looking at you. *(They look at each other)* Dr. H has offered me a job.

MARY. I thought you didn't like Dr. H.

PETER. No, I... but that's what I mean about destiny. This job. It's for an organization. A government organization.

MARY. What's it called?

PETER. It doesn't have a name yet.

MARY. What will you be doing?

PETER. I can't tell you.

MARY. Why?

PETER. Top secret.

MARY. Top secret?

PETER. Yes.

MARY. But it's important. This job. What you'll be doing.

PETER. Very.

MARY. It's your destiny.

PETER. Yes.

MARY. I hope you don't take this the wrong way, but I don't want to hear about your destiny.

PETER. But I thought... when we sat on the grass... I thought you liked me.

MARY. I did.

PETER. Thank you. Thank you.

MARY. Peter, why did you ask me here? No one else would listen? About *destiny*? Maybe it makes you better than everyone back home, to be here at Harvard having ideas about destiny. When you were little you thought you were worse than everyone, didn't you? Hovering in corners reading books, always alone, apart. But *I* didn't think you were worse. I thought you were smart. Oh, I used to dream I could be as intelligent as you! But you know something? Now that I'm here with you, I don't think you're half as intelligent as my cousin Karen. She's a housewife, a mother, that's all. She spends her day mopping the floor, playing baseball with her boys, going to Church. A life like every other woman in the world. Except when you sit with her at the dinner table and you watch the way she talks to her family, and listens, *really* listens, and her husband jokes with her, and the boys punch each other like kittens playing, and the *light* in her eyes... she loves... *every moment they give her... all* of it. Peter, that's what I want for my destiny. I don't care if I'm a housewife or a secretary or a teacher or just a good-for-nothing spinster, as long as I can have that *light* in my... And I think I can have that light if I don't have to... what my mother had to go through because she... because the first war killed Mama's father and the second one took her son. Karen didn't have to go through that. Karen never had to pretend she was fasting when there wasn't enough for dinner. Peter, my mother... and your mother too... they shouldn't have had to live the way they did. Life shouldn't have made their eyes go dull. If only we can have what Karen has, if we could just be safe, all of us, no more fear, if we could all be safe... *(she cries)*

PETER. Mary. Mary. *(Gently, he sits her down)* Cold? *(She nods. He gets a shirt from the laundry pile and wraps it around her. He considers this a moment, then gets several shirts and wraps them around her. He kneels in front of her)* That's what I was trying to explain. Your cousin Karen... Shouldn't we all live like her... everyone... And not just in our country, in every country. That's why I took this job. That's what this organization... *(he stops himself)* Mary, I believe that if everyone in every country lived like Cousin Karen... Because isn't suffering in some form or another, ultimately, the cause of all war? Dr. H talks about containment, neo-realism, diplomacy, armament as basis of negotiation. But underneath all his pragmatism, he believes what I do, I know he does — we believe that all political systems must adopt democracy... for *all* people. But there are forces who don't want democracy... dictators... and others who mean well but out of ignorance or ineffectiveness, they let systems or economies fall apart. Mary, this organization, my work, I'll be... in a sense... an invisible soldier fighting for economic and political democracy for *all* people, everywhere... fighting against the causes of suffering... *(desperate)* Do you have any idea what I'm saying?

MARY. You want us all to be happy.

PETER. Yes! That's a way of putting it. *(hangs his head)* I suppose you think that's... preposterous.

MARY. No. Beautiful.

PETER. Really?

MARY. Beautiful.

PETER. And you'll be my wife, my friend, my inspiration. Together we'll accomplish —

MARY. Your wife?

PETER. Yes.

MARY. You haven't even proposed.

PETER. I don't need to. Don't you see? Destiny!

MARY. I'm afraid you've got the wrong girl, Peter Smith. Not only will my mother insist you propose, but my father will want to know about your financial future. We can live with them until we save enough for the down payment on our own house.

PETER. We can't live with them.

MARY. Why?

PETER. My job. We won't be returning to Utah.

MARY. *What?*

PETER. Probably ever.

MARY. But our families are there. Our friends. Our Church.

PETER. There are Churches outside Utah now.

MARY. Mormon Churches?

PETER. There's even one here. It has all the meetings. *(beat)*

MARY. *(very shaken)* May I have a glass of water?

PETER. Of course. *(He runs off to get it)*

MARY. I'm still hungry too. Maybe I will have that onion.

PETER. *(from off)* Look. Matzo bread. I'm sure my roommate wouldn't mind if you had some.

MARY. What's Matzo bread?

PETER. *(entering)* Jewish food. He's Jewish.

MARY. Really?

PETER. Yes.

MARY. I never met a Jew before.

PETER. There's lots of them at school.

MARY. Any Mormons?

PETER. No. Just me.

MARY. That must be lonely.

PETER. Mary, I thought I could do it alone, but I can't. If you want me to propose, I will. *(He gets down on his knees)* Marry me, Mary. Let's make a life together. We'll both become Cousin Karen. Then we'll make the whole world Cousin Karen! I sound pretentious again. I'm sorry. I just can't believe you came here, and that you listened... that you're even considering—*(From off, a distant sound of cheering)*

PETER. You hear that?

MARY. Yes!

PETER. Germany has surrendered, Mary! It's a sign!

MARY. For what?

PETER. For us! For my work! For destiny! *Oh my God! It's happening again!* *(He means the hole in his chest. He looks square at her taking deep breaths. She goes to him, takes his hand in hers. He calms down. He smiles. In amazement—)* It's gone. *(More loud cheering. Mary goes to him, takes his hand)*

MARY. The Germans have surrendered, Peter. It's a sign. *(They move close about to kiss—lights fade)*

ACT I

Scene Two

A Hospital Room, London, August 1947

(Newsreels of post World War II, the Soviet Union expands, the Cold War begins. Lights up on a hospital bed. Peter stands next to Mary who is lying on the bed. Overlapping—)

MARY. I can't believe you're —

PETER. I said I would be —

MARY. But you are, you're —

PETER. Whatever it took —

MARY. You're really —

PETER. I knew the baby was due —

MARY. You're here —

PETER. — this was the due date —

MARY. I couldn't call you. I couldn't send you a letter —

PETER. But I couldn't get you a message —

MARY. Dr. H wouldn't let me contact you in any way —

PETER. I wanted you to reassure you —

MARY. I was calling for Mama but she's not here either.

PETER. — so you wouldn't be frightened —

MARY. I'm halfway across the world from her.

PETER. I didn't want you to be frightened.

MARY. I just can't believe you're —

PETER. *(He strokes her cheek)* But I am. I'm here. With you. *(She relaxes. Peter smiles. He takes her hand)* How long will it take?

MARY. What?

PETER. Well. *Birth.*

MARY. The nurse said it will be awhile. I mean the Sister. They call them Sisters here.

PETER. That's confusing.

MARY. They hurt, Peter.

PETER. What?

MARY. The contractions. I never felt anything like this.

PETER. Are you having one now?

MARY. No.

PETER. Good.

MARY. But I think about the next one. I'm scared.

PETER. What can I do? Tell me what to do.

MARY. Get my mind off the next one.

PETER. *(idea)* I can show you my letters! *(He takes letters out of his coat pockets)* I wrote you every night, sometimes twice. Sometimes five or six times. *(He shows a page that's covered in black censor lines)* They've been trimmed a little. You want me to read them to you?

MARY. Just tell me how you've been.

PETER. I missed you.

MARY. Tell me where you've been.

PETER. I can't.

MARY. *(crestfallen)* I know.

PETER. You read the papers?

MARY. The *Times*. The international section.

PETER. You've been following Romania?

MARY. Yes.

PETER. And a man named Maniu? Maniu's trial in particular?

MARY. Yes!

PETER. I have nothing to do with that.

MARY. *(crestfallen)* Oh.

PETER. The truth is I'm just a small cog in a vast… To be objective. Objectively, there's really no point at all to what I do. Some bureaucrat makes up tasks for me simply to justify the cost of my training.

MARY. That can't be true.

PETER. It is true.

MARY. The ladies at Church, their husbands are dentists or shopkeepers or salesmen. They're useful. But Sweetheart, what you do... it's essential. It's... Whenever I think of you I'm so proud I start hopping around the room.

PETER. You do not.

MARY. Just yesterday I hopped for a full half hour. I looked like a dancing elephant.

PETER. But a beautiful one.

MARY. A very pregnant large fat beautiful one. *(winces)*

PETER. What's wrong?

MARY. Contraction. Send in the nurse—Sister.

PETER. What for?

MARY. *(in pain)* She... distracts me...

PETER. *(eager)* But I can distract you. I'll tell you a joke! Maybe not. I'm no good at telling jokes. I know! *(Peter makes faces at Mary, but he stops when he sees this isn't distracting her. He tries doing a silly dance. But he's too self-conscious to continue. He's desperate to distract her. An idea—)* I can tell you about the dog! On the way here, I saw a dog eating out of a garbage pail. For a moment I thought he was Ralph. I never told you about Ralph. *(She moans in pain. He's even more desperate to distract her. She is in pain throughout)* Ralph wasn't my dog, I met him at a bus stop. One of my trips to visit my father. This particular morning the bus was late so I had plenty of time to think about where I was going, the asylum: Esther picking invisible rats off the floor, Jacob shouting "Number Eight! Number Eight!," my father pacing back and forth back and forth muttering "I'm sorry I'm sorry I'm sorry." Finally the bus pulled up in front of me, but I couldn't make myself get on. I just let it go by. I began to panic. What if someone saw me and told my mother I hadn't gone to visit my father. Just then a dog came up and began licking my shoe. I'd seen him before; he lived at the Granger dump. Oh boy, was he ugly. He smelled, his hair was matted, his ribs stuck out like the teeth of a fork. But his eyes, they were laughing. They made me laugh. I bought him food at a store, I named him Ralph, then I played with him in a cornfield. I taught him to sit, lie down, fetch, do somersaults. And all the time we were laughing! Night came and I walked back home. I lied to my mother, "Dad's getting better, Mom." She smiled! She did her chores singing show tunes. The next month I didn't get on the bus again, and I played in the field again with Ralph. We did this almost two years. It was my favorite day of the month. No, it was the only day. All the other days were just waiting for that one day when I could play with my dog. I never got caught. The hospital staff never asked why the visits stopped, not even when they called to say my father had died. *(Peter doesn't notice that Mary's contraction has eased off.)* I brought Ralph home after that. I wanted to keep him but Mom said we couldn't afford to feed him. She told me to have Mr. Clark at the pound put him out of his misery. *(He notices Mary. Suddenly concerned)* Are you all right now?

MARY. Did you do it?

PETER. What?

MARY. Put him out of his misery.

PETER. Yes.

MARY. But how miserable was he? Before you put him out of it.

PETER. We couldn't afford to feed him.

MARY. That's all? *(Peter nods)*

MARY. Then why didn't you take him back to the dump? He ate at the dump, right?

PETER. Mother told me to take him to the pound, so I took him to the pound.

MARY. She wasn't thinking straight. She was working two jobs. Her husband had just died in the insane asylum. You could have taken him back to the dump without telling your mother.

PETER. You want me to call the nurse, Sweetheart? You look exhausted.

MARY. I want to know! Why didn't you take your dog to the dump?

PETER. Well. I never thought about it 'til now. *(He thinks)* That option never occurred to me. *(He thinks)* Why did I take him to the pound? *(agitated)* I loved my dog. Why did I tell Mr. Clark to kill him?

MARY. *(now trying to comfort)* Shh.

PETER. I loved him!

MARY. Your Dad had just died. You weren't thinking straight.

PETER. That's no reason to kill Ralph! *(beat)* Why did I kill my own dog?! *(He considers this. Lights fade)*

ACT I
Scene Three
An Apartment, Washington D.C. 1954

(Newsreels about the rise of the Soviet Union, the Cold War, about Joe McCarthy and his accusations of American citizens. Lights up on a couch. A phone sits on a side table. The room is cluttered with toys, children's books, a broom and dust rag. Mary comes on wearing a simple white flowing robe and begins picking up toys. She picks up a toy soldier, examines it, then winds it up and lets it march around the floor. She winds up another soldier and another. They all crash into each other and fall, their legs kicking in the air. She laughs. Sound of door unlocking)

MARY. Peter? *(The door opens but is stopped by the chain lock)*

PETER. *(from off)* Mary?

MARY. You're early.

PETER. *(from off)* Yes. *(She looks around the room at the mess. A look of horror crosses her face. Then she flies into action picking up toys, but she gets too many in her arms and they all fall. The door jiggles against the chain)*

PETER. *(from off)* Mary?

MARY. Coming! *(Mary grabs the broom and sweeps the toys under the table)*

PETER. *(from off)* Something wrong? Mary?

MARY. Coming! *(She shoves the broom under the table. The head sticks out. She shoves the head in but now the handle sticks out. Pounding)*

PETER. Mary?! *(She puts a toy truck over the handle to hide it. She runs to the door and undoes the chain. But before she can open the door, Peter shoves a bouquet of flowers through. All we see is his arm and the flowers. She laughs in delight. She takes the flowers. He comes in, sets down his suitcase, kisses her and heads off toward the children's bedroom)*

MARY. *(calling after him)* Don't get them excited. They're almost asleep! *(While he's out of the room she quickly pulls down the tablecloth to hide the toys underneath. She takes the broom off. She plunks candles down on the table. She pinches her cheeks for extra color and settles herself into an appealing pose. Peter comes back. He takes her in his arms and kisses her passionately. He picks her up and heads for the bedroom)*

MARY. Peter?

PETER. Mm?

MARY. Were the children asleep?

PETER. No.

MARY. We better wait.

PETER. You're right. *(He drops her)*

PETER. Sorry! I'm sorry! Is your foot hurt?

MARY. No.

PETER. Why are the children awake anyway?! It's way past their bedtime!

MARY. It's seven o'clock.

PETER. That's way past their bedtime!

MARY. *(laughing)* It isn't way past their—

PETER. It was way past my bedtime when I was their age.

MARY. No it wasn—

PETER. I'll call my mother. She'll tell you. It was way past my bedtime.

MARY. We can't call your mother. It's not in the budget.

PETER. We call her sometimes.

MARY. Sundays. It's in the budget for Sundays.

PETER. That's right. So?

MARY. What?

PETER. What can we do? If we can't — *(gestures: make love)* What else can we do?

MARY. *(teasing)* You can explain the Korean War again.

PETER. You can tell me what did you do while I was away.

MARY. That's boring.

PETER. Not to me.

MARY. *(by rote)* I went to Church Sundays. I bought Matthew some shoes. Boring! Oh but I watched TV, the Army what-do-you-call-its. *(very upset)* I don't know what to think about Zwicker. Cohn says this, Welch says that. Imagine, they've infiltrated the Army —

PETER. Shh. What's that?

MARY. What?

PETER. Under your robe. *(She shows him a glimpse of her negligee. He is overcome)* That's… I'd like to see that without your robe… please.

MARY. *(opens her robe)* I'll take it back tomorrow if you say we can't afford it. *(He goes to her and tries to pull her robe completely off)* The children, Peter.

PETER. They must be asleep by now! They've been in there for hours!

MARY. I'll go see. *(She runs off. Peter adjusts his pants. He wipes sweat from his brow. She runs on)* Mark's still reading his book.

PETER. He can't be reading! He just turned four!

MARY. He's like you. He learns fast.

PETER. Then make him stop! He'll frighten the other children at school!

MARY. He'll be asleep soon, Sweetheart. Soon.

PETER. I hope so! Mary? What if we're very very quiet?

MARY. When have we ever been quiet?

PETER. We could try. We'll make it a game. If one of us makes the slightest sound we'll stop. *(He kisses her pushing her down on the couch, groping her energetically. But then he stops. He sits up)*

MARY. What's wrong?

PETER. *(embarrassed)* I can't.

MARY. Can't what?

PETER. You know. *(gesture: lost his erection)*

MARY. Why?

PETER. It just — *(gesture: deflated)*

MARY. But you never — *(gesture: deflate)*

PETER. I know I never… Not around you. I'm always — *(gesture: aroused)* — around you.

MARY. We can try again.

PETER. I'm not in the mood.

MARY. You're always in the —

PETER. Not tonight.

MARY. Is something bothering you?

PETER. Yes! I can't…! *(gesture: get it up)*

MARY. I mean is there something bothering you that would cause you to — *(gesture: deflate)*

PETER. Why should there be? I was happy as a loon coming home to you. *(He plops down in a chair. He considers his predicament)* Yes. *(beat)* Something bothers me.

MARY. Work? *(He nods)* Can you tell me? *(He looks at her. He considers telling her. Then he looks away)*

PETER. No. *(He looks at her again)* Maybe I'll tell you part of it anyway.

MARY. Peter, you shouldn't.

PETER. You're right. *(He broods)*

MARY. Hungry? Glass of milk? *(He shakes his head no)* You're pale.

PETER. Mary?

MARY. What?

PETER. I need your help.

MARY. You want me to dial Dr. H?

PETER. I can't talk to Dr. H.

MARY. Then there must be someone in your department you could —

PETER. No one. I can't talk to anyone. Except you.

MARY. *(tenderly)* Peter. You can't —

PETER. I've got to talk to someone.

MARY. If Dr. H finds out, he'll —

PETER. You won't tell him. You'll keep quiet. *(She doesn't know what to say. Desperate)* Just this once. Please. *(beat)* I think I'm in trouble. *(Long pause. Mary gently touches his face)*

MARY. Promise we won't do this again.

PETER. We won't do this again. *(Mary sits to listen)* I did something. Outside my mandate.

MARY. Why?

PETER. *(thinks)* I don't know. *(beat)* I interviewed someone. A man in prison. I had certain questions involving the West Berlin economy. That *was* my mandate. The interrogation ended, but suddenly the prisoner began talking as fast as he could get the words out. A story about what an SS officer, Brandt, did during the war. He insisted I report Brandt to a government Prosecutor. I told him I didn't deal with these matters, he should tell his story to the proper organization. Frankly I didn't believe him. But the prisoner wouldn't take no for an answer. He literally begged me. He told me where I might find evidence on Brandt to substantiate his claims. *(He thinks about this)* I checked a source the prisoner gave me, which led me to another, and another. I built a file on Brandt. I'm not sure why. I had no idea what to do with the file. *(beat)* Mary, what I found was even worse than the prisoner had claimed. *(pause)* Two weeks ago, on my morning walk, I saw the signal. I picked up the drop. The message was from Dr. H. "Get rid of the file," he said.

MARY. He knew about the...?

PETER. I don't know how.

MARY. Were you followed by your own...?

PETER. I must have been.

MARY. But why does Dr. H care? This isn't his field—

PETER. I know it isn't his—

MARY. Is this Brandt part of the government?

PETER. He's a leather worker. He owns a shop.

MARY. Is he some kind of source for...?

PETER. Possibly. *(He puts his suitcase on the table. He opens the suitcase. He takes out a file)*

MARY. What's that? *(He doesn't answer. He struggles with himself)* The file? *(He doesn't answer. He struggles with himself)* Brandt's file? *(He nods slightly)* But you were supposed to get rid of it.

PETER. I know.

MARY. Your instructions were to get—

PETER. I know what my—

MARY. Peter. You could be arrested.

PETER. I know.

MARY. Why didn't you get rid of it?

PETER. I'm not sure. *(He opens it)*

MARY. We'll do it now. Should we cut it up? Is that how files are gotten rid of? *(He doesn't answer)* I'll get the scissors. *(She goes off. He looks through the file)*

PETER. Mary?

MARY. *(from off)* Yes?

PETER. Will you read it?

MARY. *(from off)* Read what?

PETER. The file. *(She reenters with the scissors)*

MARY. I can't. No. *(She hands him the scissors)*

PETER. I don't think I'll do that.

MARY. What?

PETER. Cut it up.

MARY. Peter?

PETER. I don't think I'll get rid of it.

MARY. What will you do?

PETER. I'm not sure. Maybe I'll show it to someone.

MARY. Who?

PETER. Someone who might do something about it.

MARY. Who would that be?

PETER. Someone public.

MARY. You'll be charged with —

PETER. Maybe not. Leaks happen all the time. Hard to trace where they —

MARY. Dr. H knows where this comes from.

PETER. Yes.

MARY. If you're sent to jail, what happens to the rest of us?

PETER. I want you to read it. I want to know what you think.

MARY. But Dr. H told you to —

PETER. All right, yes, I'll cut it up, but look at it first.

MARY. Peter, you don't seem to know how serious this —

PETER. I know how serious —

MARY. Then you'll get rid of this right —

PETER. At least look at the photographs. Like this one. *(He tries to show her. She backs away)*

MARY. Peter. Think. Dr. H is an intelligent man. A *moral* man. He wouldn't ask you to do this unless he had a very good... He's trying to protect you from something, he must be, that's why he won't tell you the whole story. He sees the big picture and we're in the dark and I think we should have faith in —

PETER. It isn't a picture. It's a puzzle.

MARY. *What?*

PETER. I have certain clearances. I'm allowed to know this piece in order to do my job. Anderson has access to that piece, Jeffers is cleared for this one over here. None of us are allowed to see each other's pieces. For security. Which I understand, I understand security, but when does this need-to-know business, these secrets — when do secrets stop serving the nation and begin serving Dr. H?

MARY. What are you *talking* about?

PETER. Who sees all the pieces? That's what I'm talking about. Out of thousands of us who have certain clearances, how many men have access to all the information the rest of us gather? Three hundred men? Thirty? Three? I wish I knew the answer to that. And then, out of the very few men with clearances to see all the pieces, how many have the authority to put the puzzle together? Mary, decisions are being made for a whole country by Dr. H. and a handful of other men who, all by themselves, have put the puzzle together for us. But what if they pieced it together the wrong way? Who knows enough to stop them? What if they've got the wrong picture?

MARY. Peter. Sweetheart. Sit down.

PETER. Don't you see the implications, Mary? I can't question Dr. H, I can't say your policy is wrong because he'll always answer "You don't know enough to have an opinion." How many men in the whole country know enough to have an opinion? A handful of elite? Is this a democracy?

MARY. Sit with me, Sweetheart. Come on.

PETER. *No!*

MARY. Then let me feel your forehead.

PETER. You think I'm sick?

MARY. Something's wrong.

PETER. Because I've started to ask questions?

MARY. Because this isn't you. You talk as if Dr. H is a communist—

PETER. That isn't what I mean at—

MARY. Peter, you *know* these men you're talking about. We go on picnics with their families, their children play with our children. Dr. H sat at our table eating roast and potatoes and talked about making the world kinder.

PETER. Look through the file now, Mary, or I'll take it to a newspaper journalist. *(The phone rings, they're startled. Peter answers it)* Yes. *(He listens)* All right. *(He hangs up)*

MARY. Who was that?

PETER. Dr. H. He's on his way here. I'm to go in the hall with him, and talk.

MARY. What about?

PETER. He didn't say.

MARY. *(terrified)* He knows you still have the file?

PETER. Yes.

MARY. *(beat)* Peter. I want you to cut up the file now. I want you to show Dr. H that from now on, you will follow his orders. I want you to fight for your job. *(Peter looks at her. He picks up the file and the scissors)*

PETER. Hold me?

MARY. Now?

PETER. I want to hold you.

MARY. Dr. H will be here.

PETER. I want to kiss you first.

MARY. I want you to cut up the file.

PETER. You don't want to kiss me?

MARY. Dr. H is on his way right now. *(Peter puts the scissors down. He puts the file down)*

PETER. He must think this is funny. Peter the hick, the Mormon, the fool, has a bit of foolish doubt, considers for a foolish moment not doing what the great Doctor orders, is even foolish enough to believe that if he foolishly doesn't destroy the file, someone might find out what this Brandt did. Someone who actually cares. Who is not interested, as the great Doctor is, in deals and trade offs and immunity for negotiated gain. Who might actually put Brandt on trial —

MARY. What he did. It's that awful?

PETER. You can't imagine.

MARY. *(upset)* Peter. I think, if you get yourself fired, nothing will happen to this… Brandt. I think this file will disappear, whatever you try to do with it. *(Peter looks up at her. He knows she's right)* But if you do complete this assignment, do your job, do all your work wholeheartedly, impeccably, you'll be promoted. And eventually — it may take ten years, 15 years — you'll have the clout, the respect, the influence… And then it'll be your say. You will deal with issues the way you think is right — *(knocking)* So soon.

PETER. Are you behind me, whatever I do?

MARY. Peter.

PETER. Whatever the consequences —

MARY. I have my opinions.

PETER. I know you —

MARY. I want my opinions to matter.

PETER. They do. They matter. *(He looks at the file one more time. He puts it down)*

MARY. What will you say?

PETER. I don't know yet. *(He goes out the door. Mary goes to the table. She touches the scissors about to pick them up. But then she looks over at the file. She's curious. She turns away. She struggles with herself. Then she goes and picks up the file. She puts it down. She struggles with herself. She opens the file and looks. Her face goes pale. She sits down. She looks through the file. Peter comes back in)* In the mental hospital, when my Dad could think, when he was lucid, he wrote essays on paper towels from the restroom, which he'd make me read when I visited. Long unintelligible manifestoes about why we needed a four hour work day, why doctors should be free, why no man should ever fight with his wife. But he never got himself out of the loony bin to accomplish any of it. *(He looks at Mary)* You're right, Sweetheart. If I get myself fired, I'll never... I want to accomplish *so*... *(He doesn't finish the sentence. He goes out and comes back with a trashcan)*

MARY. What's this? *(She shows him a photograph)*

PETER. Tattooed skin.

MARY. From dead bodies?

PETER. He made... mementos... for certain officers... and wives...

MARY. From prisoners' bodies? *(Peter nods slightly. Mary picks up another picture)* Are these...? *(pause)* Shrunken heads? *(They consider this horror)*

PETER. *(convincing himself)* In the big picture, as I get promoted, when I have enough say, when it's *my* decision I'll put people like that on trial. I'll... But I have to stay the course. *(He takes the file from her and goes to the table. He lights a candle. But he doesn't set the file on fire yet)* Look at me?

MARY. Why?

PETER. It's happening.

MARY. The hole?

PETER. It'll go away if you look at me. *(She doesn't want to, but she looks at him)*

MARY. Is it gone? *(He doesn't answer. She doesn't want to but she takes his hand)* Peter, is it gone? *(He doesn't answer. It isn't gone. He abruptly pulls his hand away. He sets the file on fire)*

PETER. We'll make love when this is over.

MARY. I'm not really in the mood.

PETER. I'm not really either. *(He blows out the candle. They watch the file burn. He drops it in the trashcan.* BLACKOUT. END OF ACT I)

ACT II
Scene One
A Lavish Home, Washington Suburb, 1969

(Newsreels about the war in Vietnam. Lights up on Mary. She wears a black evening dress. She looks in the mirror putting on red lipstick. Sound of keys in the front door. Mary looks at the front door a moment, then grits her teeth and continues putting on her lipstick. Keys jingle and jingle; they aren't getting the door open. Then soft knocking. Finally Mary throws the lipstick down and stomps to the door. She takes a deep breath. She opens the door)

MARY. Husband! Sweetheart! So nice you dropped in. Where is it you've been? It's a rhetorical question.

PETER. *(whispers, angry)* You changed the locks?

MARY. *(loud)* It's just I can't quite squelch the impulse to ask.

PETER. Shh.

MARY. Even after all these years. *(He rolls his eyes and begins going over everything in the room for bugs — under a chair, in a lamp)* Nope. I can't quite force myself not to be curious when my husband disappears one afternoon, no warning, and doesn't turn up again for three months. Even after all these years, I can't quite force myself. *(He grits his teeth. He begins to open the phone up)* Three months, two weeks, five days and four and a half hours to be exact. The children, even after all these years, still ask every night, "Do you think Daddy's hurt? Maybe they've killed him." "I don't know," I say, even after all these years. "Top secret." *("SHH!")* What's truly remarkable is that even after all these years the children remember you at all. *(This gets to him. He yanks the bug from the phone. Mary goes to the door frame, reaches on top of it and removes a bug)* That's it. There aren't any more. *(He looks at her, puzzled)* I watched when they put them in. *(more puzzled)* I heard them in here at four one morning tripping over the furniture. It would have wakened a dead person. So I got out of bed and turned on a light for them. They were quite sweet actually. *(Russian accent)* "Ve are jus doink our job, madam." I made them hot chocolate. I hope our side isn't as clumsy with this kind of thing. Is it? *(He sets the phone down)*

PETER. You went to a lawyer.

MARY. You're spying on me now?

PETER. It gets around.

MARY. All the way to Saigon or wherever you've been? It just gets around to Saigon?

PETER. I left as soon as I heard. I have to start back tomorrow morning.

MARY. You think a night with me and I'll call off the lawyer?

PETER. We have to talk about this, Mary.

MARY. Sorry, Peter. I've got plans.

PETER. Plans.

MARY. A date.

PETER. What kind of date?

MARY. How many kinds are there?

PETER. Matthew has dates. Mark has dates.

MARY. So do I now.

PETER. In front of the children? You date in front of my chil—

MARY. The children aren't here.

PETER. Where are they?

MARY. Utah. My mother's.

PETER. You sent them there so you could date?

MARY. I sent them there so they wouldn't have to watch me pack your things. *(beat)* They're in the garage. Your things. I didn't know where to ship them. *(They look at each other. Silence)*

PETER. *(very quietly)* All right. All right. We will sit down now and talk.

MARY. I don't have time for talking. I have a date.

PETER. Then talk with me 'til he gets here. Please.

MARY. I have to get ready.

PETER. You are ready. You look beautiful.

MARY. I'm not beau—

PETER. You are. You're *truly*—

MARY. I'm ugly, Peter. But at least I'm all here. You've got a hole in you so big I could throw a chair through you, you wouldn't feel a thing.

PETER. *(stung)* You think I don't feel?

MARY. I know you don't.

PETER. How do you know?! What's your evidence?!

MARY. I don't have lab results, Peter. It's not the kind of thing that shows up in a urine test.

PETER. Give me something concrete. You can't indict me like that without some kind of basis—

MARY. I have basis coming out of my ears!

PETER. Then tell me!

MARY. I've told you and told you! I'm exhausted telling you! *(She goes back to the table to her makeup)*

PETER. Mary...

MARY. What.

PETER. Tell me again.

MARY. This time will be different?

PETER. Try it and see.

MARY. What's changed, Peter? Why would today be different than all the years—

PETER. *(desperate)* I don't want you to divorce me. *(She looks at him)*

MARY. All right. We'll test this. I'll tell you something, and if you hear it, we'll talk.

PETER. All right.

MARY. But you have to really hear it. I have to see that it affects you.

PETER. You will.

MARY. John's dog. Where did you take her?

PETER. We told John if he didn't feed and walk the thing we'd have to —

MARY. Where did you take the dog?

PETER. The Schlesinger's farm. I told you.

MARY. You took the dog to the pound, right? They put her to sleep.

PETER. The farm. Where she could run —

MARY. You frighten me, Peter.

PETER. Mary, what do you want me to say?

MARY. I think you could do anything and not feel remorse. You're that... cold. *(A beat. Then Peter yanks a stack of letters out of his jacket pocket)*

PETER. I still write you letters. Is that cold? Where are your letters to me? *(takes out more letters)* I make up stories that you're with me, that we eat dinner together by the Ou River, that we walk arm and arm through what's left of Mahaxy and make love on a bed of grass. Is that unfeeling? Where are your letters to me, Mary? How cold are you to me? Here. Read my letters. *(He tries to force letters into Mary's hands. She shoves them back)* They're from your husband. *Read them—*

MARY. No! *(quietly)* You failed the test, Peter. *(They look at each other. He's abashed. Very hurt)* Would you please go check into the Surf's Up Motel or something? I have a date tonight.

PETER. *(reaches out to her)* Mary.

MARY. Now we get Poor Penitent Peter. Sorry, I don't buy it anymore.

PETER. Can we just —?

MARY. Oh, here's Pathetic Peter. The irony is you really are pathetic, you don't have to act it.

PETER. *(humiliated)* I'm not pathetic.

MARY. You're the most pathetic person I know. *(She turns her back on him and goes back to her makeup. Silence)*

PETER. *(on the attack)* You going to introduce him to me? Your date? Peter, this is my date. Date, this is my husband.

MARY. He won't come in. He honks. I go out.

PETER. That's not very polite. What kind of date is that? You like him, this impolite date?

MARY. I like him.

PETER. Why?

MARY. He calls me every day.

PETER. Sounds dull.

MARY. He never travels.

PETER. Boring!

MARY. I like boring now.

PETER. What does he do, this boring dull impolite date of yours.

MARY. He picks me up. He drives me to a restaurant —

PETER. His *job*, Mary. What's his *job*.

MARY. Manager.

PETER. IBM? Continental Grain?

MARY. Sears.

PETER. *(rolls his eyes)* Is he Mormon?

MARY. No.

PETER. Mary.

MARY. When was the last time you were in Church?

PETER. Have you slept with him?

MARY. None of your business.

PETER. I think it is my business.

MARY. Who else have you slept with, Peter?

PETER. No one.

MARY. Right.

PETER. No one.

MARY. *(quietly)* You're away 2 months, 3 months, sometimes 6 months at a time. You've been absent half our married *life*—

PETER. Mary, that's *hyperbole*—

MARY. You're away, Peter. A *lot*. And now you have the audacity to claim you've been *faithful*?!

PETER. *(desperate)* I have been, Mary.

MARY. If you were me, would you believe that. *(they look at each other)*

PETER. Mary. Will you sit on the couch with me? Please? We won't argue. We'll be quiet.

MARY. I don't want to talk, Peter.

PETER. We won't say a word.

MARY. What are you up to?

PETER. I just want to sit on my couch with my wife before she isn't my wife anymore. *(She considers)* Just sitting. I promise.

MARY. Just 'til he gets here.

PETER. All right. *(She sits. Beat)*

MARY. You'll get a lawyer?

PETER. *(gently)* Shh.

MARY. You need your own lawyer.

PETER. No talking.

MARY. You need someone to work out your visiting rights.

PETER. Visiting rights?

MARY. For the children.

PETER. For my own...? No, I won't need a lawyer.

MARY. You think you can change my mind?

PETER. I hope I can.

MARY. Go on. Try to change it.

PETER. Mary.

MARY. You don't have any idea how you're going to do this, do you Peter?

PETER. Please. Just be quiet with me on the couch.

MARY. Until something occurs to you, right? About how to change my mind.

PETER. Will you hold my hand?

MARY. Not going to work, Peter.

PETER. I'm not trying to make anything work. I'm... *(He tries to take her hand. She pulls away)*

MARY. Most married couples, when they sit on the couch, talk about their day. The wife tells clever things the children did. The husband tells what happened in the office. What happened at the office today, Peter? Business good?

PETER. Don't.

MARY. I'm not sure what business you're in, but I remember once you said it had something to do with... What was it...? Something about happy?

PETER. Don't do this.

MARY. And now you're... I don't know of course, but I think you're in the business of war, the one in Vietnam to be specific.

PETER. Take my hand. Please.

MARY. I can't figure out how war has anything to do with happy, but I got a clue about two weeks ago at a party. You weren't there, of course, but Dr. H was, and we got to talking — he was with his latest wife and they were both drinking and jolly and he said — Dr. H said — *(German accent)* "War is good for the economy." Which may explain why we don't seem to be winning it or losing it. Ending it isn't the point.

PETER. *(laying into her)* How much real information do you have access to? Five percent of it? *Ten percent?!*

MARY. True. I'm only allowed the slightest hints of information, mostly what I get from newspapers and parties, but based on my hints of information I've developed a theory. The war will go on forever because *(German accent)* "War is good for the economy!"

PETER. I wish I could fully express what your support means to me. That I have a wife who cares about my work the way you do, who believes in my cause… who comforts me the way you do when I'm out in the world putting my life on the line so that she can have her beautiful white house and does NOT have to worry about enough to eat, does not EVEN have to worry about her sons getting killed in a war the way her mother's son was killed because between MY INFLUENCE and MY MONEY her sons don't have to go have guns and grenades and mines and bombs and chemicals fired at them THE WAY OTHER SONS DO— *(takes a breath)* I'm stopping. I've stopped. *(He's calm)* I wasn't going to do this tonight. *(Pause. Mary looks at her watch)*

MARY. He's late.

PETER. He's standing you up.

MARY. He's just late, Peter. You know what the traffic is like.

PETER. Tell him no when he gets here. Tell him something came up.

MARY. I can't do that.

PETER. Tell him you want to spend the night with your husband.

MARY. I don't want to spend the night with my husband. I want him to leave. I want to sell the house. I want to move back to Utah.

PETER. Sell the house?

MARY. Yes.

PETER. *(He takes this in)* Not the couch.

MARY. What?

PETER. Don't sell this couch.

MARY. It's old, Peter. I think we should throw it away.

PETER. We sat on this couch. We talked here. We played backgammon.

MARY. That was a long time ago.

PETER. Remember our wedding night?

MARY. No.

PETER. I sat here and just looked at you. We made love on this couch.

MARY. Not this one.

PETER. Yes.

MARY. We didn't have this one for another two years.

PETER. This one. It was a wedding present from your cousin Karen.

MARY. She gave us the punch bowl.

PETER. Remember that night we sat on this couch, you were mending something, I was reading. All of a sudden the brown afghan between us raised up and growled. Little James had been waiting under that brown afghan to surprise us. I smiled, I laughed. And I looked over at you and you were smiling too. And for a moment nothing else mattered but our children, and us, smiling together.

MARY. I remember things too.

PETER. Yes?

MARY. I remember a day a few years ago. Luke had been fighting in school. John was giving me lip. You were no help at all. You stayed in your office doing whatever it is you do to prepare for a trip. Then the phone rang. My father was dead of a heart attack. I threw myself on our bed and wailed. You came in and just stood there. Finally you said you were sorry, but wasn't it a great thing he'd lived a long life and died so painlessly. Then without touching me, without any gesture of comfort, you turned and walked out of the room. You left on your trip that night. I made up excuses for you in my head. You'd been under such pressure. You really did feel for me, you just couldn't express it the way I needed you to. That night the kids and I came home from the funeral I woke up at three in the morning. The house was silent. Which was strange, the house is usually filled with sound. I walked around in the dark listening to the silence, and each room I went into — little Mary's room, James' room, the kitchen, the hall — I wanted to see you there. I wanted to tell you how much I missed my Dad. I kept walking from room to room weeping, couldn't stop, then finally I put a photo of you on my bedside table and I talked to you 'til 7 in the morning. The next night I talked to you again and every night after that 'til you came home.

PETER. I never saw a photo there. On your side table.

MARY. I put it away.

PETER. Why?

MARY. Because when you were *finally* there, after imagining for four months what would happen when you finally came home — I thought you'd hold me and I'd tell you about the characters Dad used to do to make me laugh and you'd talk softly to me and I'd cry until all the sadness was gone. But instead you walked in and said, "Hi Mary, I'm swamped" and without a word about Dad you marched into your office and shut the door.

PETER. Mary, I had a hundred page report to write in less than two weeks — *(overlapping)*

MARY. You always have a hundred page —

PETER. Not always. There's no such thing as —

MARY. It's as if I don't exist for you anymore.

PETER. Nothing is always —

MARY. As if no one exists. We're all chess pieces! Pawns you move around the —

PETER. I'm sorry about your father, I'm sorry I didn't express —

MARY. I'm the maid piece! Or a hostess piece!

PETER. It was wrong of me not to comfort you —

MARY. Or sometimes just a piece! That's all I am to you anymore, *a piece of ass!*

PETER. You're screaming again, I can't stand how much you scream at me —

MARY. I have to scream at you, Peter! That's the only way I get through to you! I don't like that I'm a screaming ugly bitch, but that's how bad I want to get through to you!

PETER. You do get through to me!

MARY. I can't make a dent!

PETER. Loud and clear!

MARY. Like shouting into an empty cave!

PETER. You've taken all your rage at God knows what, all your frustration, all the hatred you've concocted, all the contempt you've nurtured, all your resentment — and you've made me guilty of all of it! I'm to blame for everything wrong with your world! Mary, you used to think I was a hero in some small way. You used to be proud of my work, when did that stop? You believed in me, one hundred percent!

MARY. How can I believe in you, Peter? I don't know what you're doing!

PETER. What are you accusing me of?

MARY. I don't know. You tell me!

PETER. You treat me like a criminal. I'm not a criminal, Mary!

MARY. How can I know that?!

PETER. Because I tell you!

MARY. You lie for a living, Peter. How can I believe you?

PETER. Because I ask you to! *(beat)* Let's stop, Sweetheart. I'll stop. We'll both stop.

MARY. OK. I'm stopping.

PETER. I'm stopping too.

MARY. I stopped.

PETER. OK. *(silence)* The photo. The one you talked to. Is it in the garage?

MARY. No.

PETER. You threw it away? *(Mary goes to her table where her makeup is scattered. The photo is there on the table. She's been looking at it. She picks it tenderly up and hands it to him)* I'm sorry about your father. I wish I'd…

MARY. I know. *(overlapping—)*

PETER. Sweetheart. If we could find some way to—

MARY. What?

PETER. Change or—

MARY. Is that possible?

PETER. If we could find a way to *connect*—

MARY. How?

PETER. Something—

MARY. I've tried everything—

PETER. Let me take you to Paris.

MARY. We've been to—

PETER. Like a second honeymoon. We'll start over—

MARY. Can we do that?

PETER. We can go to a counselor, a shrink.

MARY. How would that work, Peter. You're never here.

PETER. I'll try… It'll be difficult… What if I could arrange to be home more.

MARY. You'd do that?

PETER. I'll do anything.

MARY. Really? Anything?

PETER. Mary. When I heard you wanted to divorce me… We've been married 23 years. We can't…

MARY. You'd really do anything.

PETER. Yes.

MARY. Would you answer a question?

PETER. Ask.

MARY. If you won't give me an answer, then it really is over between us.

PETER. If I answer?

MARY. That would be a miracle.

PETER. I'll answer. Whatever it is. I'll do anything. *(pause)*

MARY. All right. *(pause)* What did you do?

PETER. What do you mean?

MARY. *(beat)* That night you cried. What did you do that made you cry?

PETER. I don't know what you're talking about.

MARY. Yes you do.

PETER. No.

MARY. You'd been away for seven months that time. But the night you came home you didn't hug the children. At the dinner table, you burst into tears.

PETER. I was exhausted. I told you.

MARY. It wasn't exhaustion.

PETER. I hadn't slept a full night in —

MARY. You did something when you were away. I felt it. The children felt it. The whole house seemed to go dark. What did you do that made you cry? *(pause)* You're not going to answer?

PETER. It'll blow someone's cover.

MARY. It won't leave this room. *(He can't answer)* There's no hope for us unless I know. *(pause)*

PETER. *(very difficult)* All right.

MARY. *(in wonder)* Really?

PETER. *(He thinks. He nods)* Be good to get it off my... *(pause)* OK. What I did... *(gives a laugh)* This is hard... I ah... (Silence. He struggles with *himself)* When I was five, maybe six... my mother came home one night after working two jobs. She must have been too tired to eat because when she sat down at the kitchen table she didn't touch the stew my sister had made for her. She just looked at the wall. I stood by the stove and I watched her looking at the wall, and an idea came into my head. My mother should not be sad.

MARY. Is this your answer?

PETER. *(gives a laugh)* Childish idea. But I kept hold of it, and as I grew up I added to it, developed it, about how governments could... So no one would ever have to be sad like that. I saw this as my mission, and I went into the world to accomplish it. But there came certain events, resistances, obstacles. And the attempts I made did not create the results I wanted. And I realized I was too idealistic, *unrealistic*. I saw that the world I was in was not the world I pictured as a boy. It was just not that simple. But no matter how disillusioned I became, no matter how frustrated and bitter, I still wanted to accomplish my goal. So I became pragmatic, realistic, I used whatever means necessary, including some things I didn't feel entirely good about. And the years went by and I did some pretty despicable things, but I learned to see this as my personal sacrifice. I was no longer a "good" person, I had sacrificed my "goodness," *but I began to have an effect.* Then one day I got carried away and I did something worse, perhaps, than what I'd done before and now you're asking me to tell you about it, make some kind of confession. Why? You want me to repent? Never do it again?

MARY. Yes. I want that.

PETER. My work. It's not about moral philosophy. I'm not paid to act religious. Everything I've done — including mistakes, including actions you might call unethical or immoral — I've done *everything* in service of my boyhood idea. And at some point — probably not in my lifetime — my idea will become reality. Because of *everything* I've done. *I won't repent for anything.* (honking)

MARY. He's here.

PETER. Don't go. *(She gets her purse)* Don't go!

MARY. If you're staying the night, please sleep in one of the children's rooms.

PETER. We were married in the Temple.

ACT II • SCENE ONE

MARY. I know, Peter.

PETER. You vowed you'd be with me. You made a vow.

MARY. I have to break my vow. *(She starts for the door. He blocks her)*

PETER. Look at me, Mary.

MARY. Peter.

PETER. Look at me!

MARY. Excuse me.

PETER. Why can't you look at me?!

MARY. Please get out of my—

PETER. LOOK AT ME! LOOK AT ME!

MARY. I don't want to look at you!

PETER. LOOK AT ME! *(He grabs her face)* LOOK AT ME! *(He takes her arm and throws her down on the couch)* You complain I never tell you anything. I hate that word, never. Absolutism. There is no such thing as never. For instance, right now I'm going to tell you some stuff I've learned about God. Stuff they didn't tell us in Sunday School. Stuff I had to learn the hard way. *(She tries to get up, he pushes her down)* OK, you're impatient, so I'll give you an overview. The main stuff so to speak. Which is this. God does not talk in words. The Bible, love your neighbor—that's people talking, not God. God talks in strength. If God wanted you to leave He'd make you stronger than me. *(She tries to get up, he pushes her down)* You see? Survival of the fittest, Mary. Survival of the fittest. *(She tries to get up. He gets her into an arm hold)*

MARY. You're hurting me.

PETER. That's God talking to you. He's telling you you have choices. Free will! You can keep fighting me which means you'll keep getting hurt. Or you can stop fighting, go passive, stop caring, which means you'll be trampled, squashed. Or. You can become like me. Which is it, Mary? *(Knocking. They both look up. Mary struggles to get free)*

MARY. *(calling)* Just a minute!

PETER. Choice one. The fight. *(He tightens his arm hold)*

MARY. Ow! *(She stops struggling. She calls)* Something came up, OK? I can't go tonight. OK?

PETER. Choice two. Passive submission. *(more knocking)*

MARY. *(in pain)* GO AWAY!... What do I have to... do... to be like you?

PETER. Good choice! *(He lets her go)* First, I'm the strongest one here, so if you're loyal to me, if you do what I say, you automatically glean some of my strength. Second, reveal nothing. Strength is built on secrets. I may have a hole in my chest but if they don't know about it, how can they use it against me? Third, find out their secrets and use them against them. Fourth — *(He grabs her again, pulls her arm straight back and twists her hand. She grimaces in pain)* The trick isn't to stop feeling the pain. The trick is to stop minding it. And then you're free. There's nothing you won't do. *(She looks at the door. She looks up into his eyes. Slowly her face becomes blank, smooth. Now there's pounding on the door. Neither of them move. Their eyes are locked. She doesn't mind the pain. Lights fade)*

ACT II
Scene Two

A Hospital Room Waiting Room, Salt Lake City, November 1983

(Newsreels about the Reagans, the escalation of Cold War, and the 1983 bombings in Beirut. Lights up on two chairs, a side table between them and a lamp. Magazines are strewn on the table. Mary sits, Peter stands over her holding two cups of take-out coffee. Overlapping—)

MARY. *(angry)* I can't believe you're —

PETER. I'm here. I'm —

MARY. I can't believe it. I thought you were —

PETER. I said I'd be here and I'm —

MARY. I called you. I sent messages —

PETER. I knew the baby was due, this was the due date —

MARY. I told you I don't want you here, Peter. I told you I didn't want you to —

PETER. So I dropped what I was doing. I found a plane scheduled to —

MARY. Dr. H said he gave you the message —

PETER. And I was able to get on it. Allen helped with the paperwork —

MARY. How did you get here so fast anyway? You were halfway across the world. I think. I don't know of course, but with all that barracks bombing going on I'm guessing you'd be in Beirut.

PETER. I just said.

MARY. Said what?

PETER. How I got here. I knew the baby was due soon. I got on a plane. *(pause)*

MARY. You're not even supposed to be in the same room with me. You signed a paper that said you wouldn't be in the same room.

PETER. I'll go find another room. *(goes)*

MARY. No. *(He stops)* Don't bother. I mean. As long as…

PETER. I better be legal.

MARY. Matthew said if you did show up… he wants you… here… with me. So we can get news together.

PETER. Oh, well then. If Matthew wants —

MARY. But we can't argue. That's what he said. He doesn't want us to argue.

PETER. OK. We won't argue.

MARY. OK. *(Silence. They look front)*

PETER. Everything all right?

MARY. Fine. I've never been happier.

PETER. I mean with our daughter-in-law. Matthew's wife? Susan?

MARY. Her blood pressure's high. They'll let us know if they have to do a caesarean.

PETER. Matthew's in with her?

MARY. Helping her breathe. Fathers stay for the whole event now.

PETER. That's different.

MARY. Yes. *(He hands her a coffee. She takes it)* There are magazines if you need something to read.

PETER. *(picks one up)* Got one. Thanks. *(He looks down reading his magazine. She watches him. Silence)* You?

MARY. What?

PETER. Magazine?

MARY. *(picks one up)* Got one. *(She looks down. He looks down. Silence)*

PETER. Our first grandchild.

MARY. Yes. *(She reads. He looks at her)* What?

PETER. I'm trying to remember the last time we saw each other.

MARY. Not since—

PETER. No, not since—

MARY. And that was such a—

PETER. I've been through ordeals in my life, but that took the… and that what's-his-name, that lawyer you sicked on me, Jensen?

MARY. Johnson.

PETER. Did he remind you of Dr. H?

MARY. No.

PETER. He reminded me of Dr. H. Maybe it was the glasses.

MARY. I don't think we should be talking about this.

PETER. Why not?

MARY. It might start us arguing.

PETER. Oh. Yes. Well. How are —?

MARY. Fine. Good. You?

PETER. All right.

MARY. I'm glad. *(She goes back to reading)*

PETER. That's not what I hear.

MARY. What?

PETER. That you're fine. I hear you've been drinking.

MARY. That isn't your bus —

PETER. Some incident with your car and a tree.

MARY. I cut back.

PETER. Good.

MARY. I don't drink like that anymore.

PETER. Seeing anyone?

MARY. None of your bus —!

PETER. Just trying to make conversation. Could be a long wait. Are you?

MARY. Yes. I'm seeing someone.

PETER. Serious?

MARY. No.

PETER. Sears?

MARY. Long gone. You?

PETER. Yes I date. No nothing serious.

MARY. Well I hope something works out for you.

PETER. Do you?

MARY. Yes, I sincerely hope you find someone right for you.

PETER. I don't believe that's going to happen.

MARY. You never know.

PETER. Even more now. I believe that. Now that I've been dating. Dating has taught me to believe even more that you get one chance. One person. You know. Destiny. And if you blow it, well…

MARY. I'm sorry you feel that way. *(She goes back to reading. He keeps looking at her)*

PETER. I can't tell.

MARY. What?

PETER. Your drinking doesn't show on your face.

MARY. I cut back.

PETER. You said.

MARY. I'm very strict.

PETER. You look —

MARY. Don't.

PETER. You do. You're *beauti—*

MARY. I'm not. No.

PETER. You just keep getting more… Maybe I forgot. What you look like. We haven't seen each other since —

MARY. Peter? *(She says this tenderly as if she wants to connect)*

PETER. What?

MARY. Nothing.

PETER. Tell me.

MARY. Nothing.

PETER. It's not nothing. Tell me.

MARY. No. *(She turns away from him)*

PETER. You know what you look like right now? You look exactly like you did the night I got my diploma. Remember how we went down to Boston Bay, to the Aquarium and we watched the seals? We both held my diploma with both hands — four hands holding onto that thing, it's a miracle we didn't wreck it — and we sat on that bench and watched the seals dive and swim and leap up out of the water? *(She looks in his eyes)* And now we'll have a granddaughter.

MARY. Or a grandson.

PETER. One or the other.

MARY. Yes. *(A beat. She looks away. He looks away)*

PETER. Dr. H… he believes in destiny now too. He was eating a sandwich when he told me. Crumbs were falling all over his… He still pines for his first wife. He told me that. He married all those other women hoping they'd turn out to be her. I feel sorry for him. A man his age finally realizing the one true love in his life was his first wife. *(silence)* I'm not in Beirut. I'm in Honduras, a jungle.

MARY. Aren't you breaking the rules, telling me this?

PETER. On the way here, on the plane, I wrote a letter of resignation. I'll let you read it if you want. It's a confession really. The beginning of repentance. I'll mail it, if you'll go out to dinner with me. My bargaining chip. I'll mail the letter. You can come with me, we'll mail it together —

MARY. If I…

PETER. Sweetheart, let's mail it together. *(Silence. They look in each other's eyes)*

MARY. Could you really…?

PETER. Yes. I can. You…? *(silence)*

MARY. I'm sorry. This was a mistake. I have to tell Matthew. I can't believe you're even suggesting —

PETER. Proposing.

MARY. As if anything would be different between us! As if your behavior, my reactions… And even if it could, don't you think… after all the… don't you see it's too late?

PETER. Is it?

MARY. Would you do me a favor? Would you stay away. Please. Weddings, funerals, births — we'll both have to attend them but please don't talk to me or look at me or if possible come into the same room. If you care about me at all, please do this for me!

PETER. All right.

MARY. I'm sorry. I honestly thought we could sit in the same room. I'll go explain it to Matthew. *(She exits. Peter watches her go. Lights fade)*

ACT II
Scene Three

An austere apartment, Washington D.C. 1993.

(In black, CNN news about the fall of the Berlin wall, the end of the Cold War, the first World Trade Center bombing. Lights up on a messy apartment—piles of clothes, books and papers. A mop in a bucket leans against a wall. Peter sits in a wheelchair. There's a thick manuscript on his lap. He talks on the phone)

PETER. You don't understand—*(listens)* But you don't understand—*(listens)* But Sam Hart's book kept you in the publishing business for the next five years. There's no evidence mine wouldn't do the same thing. *(listens)* I know how long ago that was. *(listens)* Let me tell you a story. One that's not in the book. It's 1964. Knopf was going to publish a book about me even though it would have blown the cover on several vital projects, so I called Dr. H and the book never saw the light of day. Oh, and two Knopf editors were immediately fired. *(listens)* No I'm not trying to bully—*(listens)* I'm not trying to threaten you! The point of the story is to show you the kind of power I once had which I think is fascinating, which I think will sell my book! *(listens)* I know it's not 1964! That's not the point of the story! *(listens)* I'm sorry I yelled. I didn't mean to yell. No please don't hang up on me I didn't mean to—*(The phone has gone dead. He slams it into the receiver, then picks it up again, dials)* Hi Jane. I gotta talk to Dr. H. *(listens)* Come on, Jane. He didn't say that. *(listens)* Never? You're not supposed to put me through ever? *(listens)* He must have meant it as a joke. *(listens)* That doesn't even sound like his words. He doesn't put words together like that. *(The door opens. Mary comes in with a small suitcase. She wears a soft, flowing dress and holds a hat with flowers. Peter sees Mary. His jaw drops)*

MARY. You left your door unlocked.

PETER. Mary?

MARY. You shouldn't leave your door unlocked. It isn't safe. *(Peter is absolutely dazed)*

PETER. I…

MARY. What?

PETER. Thought I locked it.

MARY. Well you didn't. May I come in?

PETER. Please. Please. Why do you even ask?

MARY. I thought you wouldn't want me to.

PETER. Why wouldn't I want you to?

MARY. Well.

PETER. Oh. But that was years ago. Years. *(beat)*

MARY. Is someone still on?

PETER. Hm?

MARY. The phone, Peter.

PETER. Oh. Oh yeah. *(into the phone)* I have to go. My wife just—

MARY. Ex-wife.

PETER. *(into the phone)* Ex-wife just… I have to go. *(hangs up)* Well.

MARY. Yes.

PETER. I can't believe you're here.

MARY. Well I am.

PETER. Oh I'm sorry. Have a seat. Please. *(He takes a pile of laundry off a chair so she can sit down, but then he doesn't know what to do with the pile. Finally he just drops it on the floor)* Sorry about the mess. I thought about hiring a cleaning man but I decided I couldn't afford him.

MARY. *(smiles)* I took all your money.

PETER. Yes… But that was years ago. *(awkward pause)* Are you hungry? I haven't got much. There's some chicken, oranges. Cheese?

MARY. Water. I'll get it.

PETER. But you're the guest.

MARY. But you're — *(She gestures to the wheelchair)* Kitchen? *(He nods. She goes off)*

PETER. There's milk! Want some milk?

MARY. *(from off)* No thank you.

PETER. *(beat)* I just can't believe you're here. *(beat)* Why are you here? *(He listens)* Mary? *(listens)* Why did you come here?

MARY. *(re-enters)* I have something to ask you.

PETER. What? *(pause. She thinks)*

MARY. We could talk first, couldn't we? Catch up? It's not as if the world's about to end.

PETER. All right. You start.

MARY. No, you.

PETER. I know. We'll be quiet. Sit here quietly. Eventually one of us will know what to say.

MARY. All right. *(They sit. She starts to say something, but then changes her mind. Then he starts, but then changes his mind. Finally —)*

PETER. We could talk about the children!

MARY. Yes, the children.

PETER. They all call. They tell me about you.

MARY. They tell me about you too.

PETER. Especially Matthew. Long phone calls. Hours.

MARY. Yes, he's always been —

PETER. Longwinded. Like me.

MARY. Well. Yes.

PETER. Did he tell you about this? *(He means the wheelchair)*

MARY. Some.

PETER. The doctors say it's all in my mind and I know it's all in my mind but that doesn't stop the sensation. Sometimes I feel there's nothing left of me but my legs, my hands and my head. And sometimes, without the part of me in the middle, I feel my feet start off somewhere and leave my head behind completely.

MARY. That must be difficult.

PETER. Not half as difficult as when my head decides to go one way, my feet another and my hands a third direction entirely. I end up scattered all over the room. That's why I'm in this chair. It's an organizing principle. Of course I know all that doesn't really happen, but still I like to avoid the sensation.

MARY. Is it happening now?

PETER. No.

MARY. Good. *(pause)*

PETER. You never married again.

MARY. Neither did you.

PETER. You live with your cousin. With Karen.

MARY. Yes. They made you retire.

PETER. Matthew told you what happened?

MARY. A lot of it.

PETER. Wasn't pretty.

MARY. No. That your book?

PETER. This?

MARY. Matthew said you wrote your memoirs.

PETER. I haven't signed a contract yet but there's some serious nibbles. It's very entertaining, my book, I made sure it was very entertaining. Even told about Castro's beard.

MARY. Castro's beard?

PETER. A vital part of his image, his beard. Symbolized strength, revolution. John and Dan figured if they could ruin it he'd look ridiculous to the Cuban people. So they came up with a plan to sprinkle his shoes with a woman's depilatory. It would get on his hands when he put on his shoes and then he'd touch his face. The plan fell through, but it's a good story. Here's another one. In the Philippines, George, Larry and Mike drained blood out of corpses, fixed them up to look like vampires had gotten to them, and left them on the beach. Sure sell, this book, it just needs the right... What they say to you, editors... "Books like yours aren't in anymore, no one cares." Things like that. One woman (well she couldn't have been more than 25) one little girl rather well she was hardly little, she was fat, maybe 300 pounds, and acne, she still had acne. She said, "Mr. Smith? You're a cliché." And then she finished her lunch: jello and cottage cheese, she's on a diet. She didn't take me out to a restaurant, she didn't even order up. She put me in a little chair at the foot of her desk and made me watch her eat her lunch. I wanted to yell, tell her off, but instead I started thinking about jello. Remember Church dinners? There was always jello. And those organization luncheons. Jello salad of one kind or another. Buffets, PTA meetings, social events, there's a lot of jello. That's what I was thinking about sitting there watching this fat little acned girl eat her jello, her jaws moving, sucking. I thought of all the people I'd ever seen eating jello: red jello, green jello, yellow jello, all of America eating jello while I was in a jungle in Laos, torrential rains, trying to get 4 men off a hill before they were killed but knowing I couldn't. Or stuck for 3 weeks in a wine cellar in Beirut listening to gunfire just outside. And the people I did this for, the country, the democracy I did this for, they don't want to hear about it! Even my own organization! We do things differently now, they say. They call me immoral! Power hungry! They let Congress question me, the press ridicule me! They say I'm a mistake, an embarrassment, and then they tell me to go home, find a Church dinner and eat jello! *(pause) Without even a thank you?! (pause)* I didn't mean to go into all that. I meant to... *(pause)* You think you can ask me now?

MARY. What?

PETER. Your question?

MARY. Not yet.

PETER. My organization, all the agencies, they've all gone to hell now the cold war is over. Funding cut. People laid off. People like me who know the KGB's nothing compared to what's out there now. What's only started to come at us.

MARY. What's out there now?

PETER. *(He thinks)* Suffering. *(He thinks)* That's armed to the teeth.

MARY. I guess it's not your problem anymore.

PETER. No. I guess it isn't. *(pause)*

MARY. I think I'm ready to ask the question.

PETER. Good.

MARY. Here it is. *(Silence. She broods)*

PETER. Mary?

MARY. OK. I wanted to know... *(She broods again)*

PETER. *(finally)* Know what?

MARY. OK... Will you help me tell the children?

PETER. Tell them what?

MARY. I've got liver cancer. Advanced. It feels right to me that you help me tell the children. *(Silence. Peter is stricken)* Everything's arranged. My finances. Karen will take care of me. Everything's in order. *(beat)* Except one thing. One thought. *(beat)* I wonder why you married me.

PETER. I loved you, Mary.

MARY. But what do you mean by love? I don't know what it means. I used to think I did... When little Matthew was just born, the way his smile took up half his face, I thought that was — Or the nights when we lay side by side holding hands and talking till we fell asleep. I thought that was — Or when we were first married, and you were coming home from your first long trip and to celebrate I decorated our little 3rd story apartment with welcome home signs and covered our bed with pink balloons. And you pushed the balloons off the bed and made love to me, but in the morning there were balloons all over, we couldn't get to the bathroom without stumbling on them, so we opened a window and tossed them all out. It was drizzling that morning, and gray. People were walking fast down the street on their way to work. And when they saw pink balloons dropping from the sky they looked so surprised and baffled it made us laugh. And I looked at you tossing balloons out the window and laughing, I loved you with such… I thought my life with you was going to be a *beautiful adventure*. And it was for a while. It was just… *beautiful*. But then, step by step, it all turned ugly. I learned that love isn't practical, isn't efficient, that Jesus is nothing more than stupid sentiment, that human beings aren't humane at all, that they are worse than starving dogs tearing at each other… *(pause)* When I finally left you and went back to Utah, I thought I could learn to see what was sweet in the world again, what was lovely. But I couldn't, Peter. My eyes were different. They had changed! I'd watch Cousin Karen tend her garden, and I wanted to see the good in her, but I couldn't, I'd see her as mean-spirited, as withered. I wanted to see the love in my mother's face, but all I saw was bitterness. *(pause)* For a long time, I kept hoping something would happen, maybe I'd even fall in love again, something, and my eyes would change back. For a long, long time I kept hoping. *(weeping)* And now, that's all I think about. I drive myself nuts. My time's almost up. What if that something doesn't happen? What if, right up 'til the last moment of my life, *the whole world looks like a mean, starving dog.*

PETER. Mary. I'm so…

MARY. I don't like my eyes like this, Peter. I want them changed back. *(She cries. Peter gets up from his wheelchair, reaches up to stroke her hair but then thinks better of it. Instead he flies into action shoving books under the table. He takes a blanket and throws it over the table like a tablecloth. He picks up the mop and bucket, but it spills. There's now a little lake of water on the floor. He takes a shirt and puts it over the lake. He shoves the mop under the table. The mop head sticks out on the other side so he covers the handle with a shirt. He picks up Mary's hat, rips a paper flower from it, sticks the flower in a glass and plunks it on the table. Then he looks at his manuscript. He considers it a moment. Then he picks up his manuscript)*

PETER. Mary? *(She looks up. She is spent)*

MARY. Your book?

PETER. Yeah. (*He throws the manuscript in the air. Pages fall all over like snow*)

MARY. You're throwing it away?

PETER. Yeah. (*pause*) Mary? Will you go out with me? On a picnic. There's a deli down the street, we can buy pears.

MARY. I don't know. It's...

PETER. There's a park nearby. There's a hill. We'll sit on the grass and eat pears.

MARY. Maybe later, Peter. I'm tired. I don't know why.

PETER. Then sleep. You can lie down on my bed.

MARY. I'm not sick. It's not that.

PETER. Or the couch. You can sleep on the couch.

MARY. Just tired. I don't know why. It just came over me.

PETER. You can rest on the couch.

MARY. I think I will lie down. (*She goes to the couch. Peter helps her. She lies down*) Our old couch.

PETER. Maybe when you wake up we can go on the picnic. Or here, if you're still tired, we can have the picnic here.

MARY. Maybe. We'll see. I think I have to sleep now.

PETER. Good. Sleep. (*A beat. He sits next to her on the couch watching her*)

MARY. I'm not sick. You don't have to watch me.

PETER. I know. (*He takes her hand in his. She doesn't protest. Her eyes fall closed. But then she reaches up and pats his chest*)

MARY. Is it happening?

PETER. It stopped when you came in. *(LIGHTS FADE OUT)*

END OF PLAY

Costumes, Set Pieces and Props

- **ACT I SCENE ONE:** A student garret, Cambridge, Mass., April 1945

Costumes:
Peter — Harvard graduate student
Mary — just in from Utah, her best suit, coat, hat, purse

Set pieces and props:

table	washcloth
2 chairs	bucket with water
academic books: political science	mop
papers: typewritten & handwritten notes	glass with daisy
	suitcase
clothes (laundry)	can of sardines
frayed quilt	fork

- **ACT I SCENE TWO:** A hospital room, London, 1947

Costumes:
Peter — coat, hat, suit
Mary — loose nightgown, pregnant prosthesis

Set pieces and props:
A hospital bed; letters, black censor lines on them

- **ACT I SCENE THREE:** An apartment, Washington, D.C., 1954

Costumes:
Peter — coat, hat, suit
Mary — robe, negligee

Set pieces and props:

couch	suitcase
coffee table	candles
phone	matches
toys	flash paper
toy soldiers	trash can
broom	file filled with photographs and typed papers
bouquet of flowers	
briefcase	scissors

- **ACT II SCENE ONE:** A lavish home, a Washington suburb, 1969

Costumes:
Peter — jeans, smart casual
Mary — black cocktail dress, purse

Set pieces and props:

couch	phone
coffee table	4 bugs (listening devices)
lamp	framed photograph
table	letters
makeup	

- **ACT II SCENE TWO:** A hospital waiting room, Salt Lake City, Utah, 1982

Costumes:

Peter — jeans, smart casual
Mary — smart casual, purse

Set pieces and props:

2 waiting room chairs	magazines
magazine table	2 coffee cups
lamp	

- **ACT II SCENE THREE:** An austere apartment, Washington, D.C., 1993

Costumes:

Peter — frayed sweater, baggy pants
Mary — soft flowing dress, hat with flowers, purse

Set pieces and props:

couch	bucket	phone
clothes (laundry)	frayed blanket	suitcase
books	wheelchair	glass
papers	manuscript	
a mop	trash can	

American Girls
by Hilary Bettis

American Girls was originally produced Off Broadway at 45th St. Theatre in New York City. The original cast was as follows: Hilary Bettis as *Amanda*, Kira Sternbach as *Katie*, Traci Hovel as *Dr. Opal Banks*. Mara Kassin understudied. *Pastor Jim* was not in the original draft. The play was directed by Jeff Cohen. The play was produced by Patrick Blake, Jeff Cohen and Adam Hirsch. The production stage manager was Michal V. Mendelson and the assistant stage manager was Rachel Hip-Flores. Costume design was by Gail Cooper-Hecht, set design by Ryan Kravetz, lighting design by Evan Purcell, video design by Gray Winslow, and PR by David Gersten.

This play is dedicated to three people: Adam Hirsch, you will be missed and loved for the rest of my life; Meir Ribalow, your generosity and passion continue to amaze me; and Romulus Linney, your friendship and honesty constantly inspire me. Without the three of you the doors may never have opened.

A special special thank you to Kira Sternbach who has traveled this journey with me since day one. Your talent, drive, passion and loyalty are rare in a human being. I love you dearly.

Many people have come and gone over the course of over forty drafts and four years of this play. For their contributions I am deeply grateful. I must give a special thank you to Patrick Blake for believing in me. I must also acknowledge Traci Hovel, Michal V. Mendelson, Ean Sheehy, Angela Astle, Mark Woods, Jan Buttram, New River Dramatists, and the ladies at Flashdancers, Private Eyes and New York Dolls for their stories and inspiration.

Cast of Characters

AMANDA   KATIE   PASTOR JIM

Characters who are prerecorded but do not appear live on stage:
FRANK MILLER   DR. OPAL BANKS

Characters whose voices we hear:
MR. BRANBALT   AN IRATE STRIPPER   A STRIP CLUB DJ   KIDS

Act I

The last day of middle school in a suburban town in Iowa, USA. Early Summer 2008

Act II

The end of Summer 2008. The interview and last scene occur two years later in Fall 2010.

Note in production: All the video except the talk show should look like a home video of amateur quality. All stage directions are written by the playwright and should be treated the same as the text.

ACT I

Video Montage One

This is all projected on a video screen. Pop music plays and images of celebrities flash across the screen faster and faster and faster until the images all blur together. BLACK OUT.

Amanda's Bedroom

The walls are decorated with posters of celebrities and tropical locations. There is a large poster of the Hollywood Sign over her bed and above that is a cross. The bed is neatly made with several stuffed animals on top of a floral comforter. Everything in the room is meticulous and outfitted with all the latest gadgets.

It is obvious these girls come from a suburban middle class family. AMANDA, *14, and* KATIE, *14, are both frumpy and awkward teenage girls. Katie wears oversized clothes and doesn't comb her hair. Amanda wears glasses, a retainer, and a pink Hello Kitty headband.*

AMANDA. This is my bed… and above that is my wonderful collection of posters. I really wish I was in Hollywood right now. *(She focuses the camera on the Hollywood poster.)* And that's Katie… Smile. What's wrong with you? Why can't you humor me?

KATIE. I'm gonna kill your dad for getting that for you! *(Katie makes faces at the camera.)*

AMANDA. Why? Jealous cause I get cool things for my birthday and you don't? *(Katie flips her off.)* Don't flip me off! Say something!

KATIE. Hi.

AMANDA. Now do something!

KATIE. Like what?

AMANDA. I don't know… Something funny.

KATIE. I'm not very funny.

AMANDA. Yes you are. You make me laugh all the time. *(Amanda puts her arm around Katie while holding the camera at a distance.)* This is my best friend Katie!

KATIE. This is my best bestest friend Amanda—

AMANDA. And I love her so much and I would do anything for her— Ewwwww did you just lick my face!?

KATIE. No.

AMANDA. You're so weird!

KATIE. I'm booooorrrred! Let's find something fun to do!

AMANDA. You can never be content can you? She's crazy. What do you want to do?

KATIE. I don't know.

AMANDA. OK… We could maybe get my mom to drive us to the movies?

KATIE. We always go to movies… *(Katie turns on the computer.)* Let's find something new! *(She looks at the camera.)* Will you turn that thing off? Please! *(Katie tries to cover the camera with her hand.)* I hate cameras! Please, Amanda!

AMANDA. Fine. *(END VIDEO MONTAGE.)*

Scene One

Amanda's Bedroom. Moments later. The girls are awkwardly dancing to loud pop music and making faces at themselves in the mirror. Katie takes out a tube of red lipstick, puts it on, and pretends like she is making out with herself in the mirror. The girls are trying to be sexy and grown-up, but they come across as childish and silly. Amanda pulls her shirt up and ties it in a knot so that it reveals her stomach. The entire time the girls are singing along to the song they dance to.

AMANDA. Do you think I look fat?

KATIE. No!

AMANDA. Promise?

KATIE. Yes! *(Katie starts to crawl around on the floor trying to be sexy, but she looks more like a toddler. Amanda starts to laugh.)*

AMANDA. That's not how you do it! *(Amanda gets down on all fours and swings her head hitting Katie in the face with her hair. Katie grabs Amanda and pulls her on the ground. Both girls are hysterical.)*

KATIE. This is gonna be the biggest bestest summer ever!

AMANDA. I know! But we have to make a secret pact so no one at school finds out and tries to copy us! *(The girls spit on their pinkies and latch them together. Overlapping.)* I've got Jesus! Yes I do! I've got Jesus! How 'bout you?

KATIE. I've got Jesus! Yes I do! I've got Jesus! How 'bout you? *(Amanda jumps up suddenly.)*

AMANDA. We have to have a name for our group like The Pussycat Dolls! Or Destiny's Child!

KATIE. Ohmigosh, ohmigosh, ohmigosh! OK… *(Both girls think for a moment.)* Pussycat Childs?

AMANDA. No stupid...

KATIE. I don't know... Girls for Jesus?

AMANDA. For a dance competition?

KATIE. But we are girls for Jesus.

AMANDA. I know, but it has to be catchy...

KATIE. Hmmm... *(Katie pulls out several Pixie Sticks, tears the paper off and pours the sugar into her mouth. Amanda does the same.)*

AMANDA. Pixie Chicks! *(Katie squeals in approval with a mouth full of blue sugar.)*

KATIE. Ohmigosh, but this is like a serious competition so we have to have a dance routine and matching outfits or something...

AMANDA. I didn't even think of that...

KATIE. I bet my sister has stuff! I'll go through her room when she least suspects it.

AMANDA. OK! And we can get some glitter glue —

KATIE. And sequins —

AMANDA. And top hats and canes with glitter! Or tiaras?

KATIE. Yeah! *(The girls jump up and down in their new discovery. Amanda grabs a piece of paper printed from the internet and studies it. She freezes.)* What's wrong? Amanda?

AMANDA. Nothing.

KATIE. What?

AMANDA. How much money do you have?

KATIE. Fifty dollars from three months of baby-sitting. I'm saving for a digital camera. Why?

AMANDA. I have fifty dollars in birthday money and another thirty from allowance...

KATIE. Why?

AMANDA. Hand me my phone. *(Katie does. Amanda dials a number.)* Hey, Josh, this is Amanda from down the street... Umm... You gave me your number... When you mowed the lawn that one time and you said since I'll be in high school next year I'll probably get beat up and I can call you... Yeah the one with the retainer... I have a question for you...

Youth Group Lesson One

Flashback. A handsome, All-American man, PASTOR JIM, 35, dressed in slacks and a polo shirt stands in the center of the stage talking to the audience. The restless voices of middle school kids fill the room. Pastor Jim waits patiently for them to settle down.

PASTOR JIM. Hey guys. All right everyone settle down. Hey, boys in the back, yes I am looking at you, Rob and Jake, settle down and stop pinching Kylie. She obviously doesn't like it. Or she might like it, in which case you should definitely stop! So the end of middle school is coming up, huh? You guys are gonna be in high school next year. Wow. I'm getting so old! You guys make me feel ancient! I am so proud of all of you guys! And this is it for us. Our last session together. Our last session... Next year, you guys will be with the grown-ups. You guys won't need me anymore... *(He gets a little choked up for a moment.)* I swear I'm not gonna cry, because I know Rob, over here, won't let me live it down! We've had a lot of fun together. Bible retreats, dances, a carnival, a kick ball tournament... We've shared a lot of fun times and good laughs in this room. But today is serious, guys. Today you guys are gonna become grown-ups in the eyes of God. So I want everyone to close your eyes. Close them tight. Amanda, no peeking. *(Pastor Jim dims the lights.)* When I was a little boy my family took a vacation to Colorado. We visited this place called Cave of the Winds. These incredible mineral formations called stalactites and stalagmites towered through the walls of this amazing creation of God's. So of course my family had to take a tour of the cave! A guide led us through narrow passageways and steep stairs and winding tunnels. My older brother Todd and I were full of confidence and excitement. We weren't scared of anything! Not bats or spiders or Indian legends about ghosts. We skipped through those passageways like we were kings of the cave! The steeper the steps the bolder we grew. The more narrow the tunnels the more we wanted to conquer them. The guide led us deeper and deeper and deeper into this massive structure. At one point, an older lady on the tour got really scared and told the guide we were going too far and she wanted to turn back. So Todd, with this calm smile, took the woman by the hand. She clutched on tightly to Todd and we continued on our journey. Then, with no warning, the guide turned out all the lights that had been illuminating our path. Everyone froze with fear! I clutched on to Todd's other hand and the lady he had helped began to whimper. There were screams and sniffling. We were a good mile deep into this cave with no sign of an exit. We had trusted this guide without question for our safety, but he had led us down this path of darkness. Then the guide said, "Many explorers ventured farther than us into this cave never to return. Their lanterns burned out or they ran out of supplies or they got so lost in the winding tunnels that they could never find their way back out. Many people perished in this cave. Listen quietly to the silence and imagine what that would be like." *(Pastor Jim takes a moment to let the kids listen to the silence.)* Listen to the silence, guys. Imagine being so far into this huge cave with no light or supplies or friends. You can scream at the top of your lungs and only bats and spiders can hear you. Listen guys… The guide went on, "After a day or two you'd slowly start to go insane from the oppressive loneliness. You'd go blind. Then you'd starve or die of thirst. This happened to many people. So we turn out the lights to remember them." After a few moments of silence someone shouted that he was going insane and to turn the lights back on. The guide laughed and, with a flick of the wrist, illuminated our path and led us back out of the darkness. That darkness is Hell, guys. Could you imagine an eternity in that cave? It would kill me guys, it would kill me if that happened to any one of you. So how do we stay in the light, guys? How do we secure our place in Heaven?

Video Montage Two — Middle School Hallway

The girls are walking down the school hallway. Katie wears oversized clothes and doesn't comb her hair. Amanda wears glasses, a retainer, and a pink Hello Kitty headband.

AMANDA. The last day of eighth grade! I am so not going to miss this place! Wave good-bye to our lockers! *(Katie waves. She sees Rob walk by. The camera never sees Rob.)*

KATIE. Rob is soooooo hot!

AMANDA. Will you get over him already?

KATIE. Someday I'm gonna make him wish he had asked me out instead of Kylie—

AMANDA. You keep telling yourself that.

KATIE. If I had done that pageant I so would have beat her… Hey! Have you heard from Josh yet?

AMANDA. Shhh… Not yet. *(END OF VIDEO MONTAGE.)*

Scene Two

The middle school cafeteria. Amanda is sitting by herself eating her lunch and texting on her cell phone. A few moments later Katie enters.

KATIE. So today Mr. Branbalt walks into homeroom and he looks at us and he says he's doing a survey just out of curiosity, he says directly to me "What are the best things in the world?" And I had to think for a minute and Kylie kicked the back of my chair because, I guess, I'm taking too long — and I really don't know what her problem is — and anyway all these things are going through my head like Jesus, my family and friends and you, of course, and food, a house, health, new clothes, HBO, you know clichéd stuff like that. And then I realize I have all of those things and I'm still not happy. Like I still feel like there is a missing piece… And then it hits me! The best thing in the world would be fame! And not just, you know, recognition for a job well done, but REAL fame! I wanna be a household name with little girls growing up worshiping me and women comparing themselves to me and men wanting me! And of course with fame comes a lot of money and good looks and a mansion and stuff. So that was my answer. To be famous. Then Kylie blurts out a laugh and whispers in my ear "you'll never amount to much." I really hate that girl!

AMANDA. She's just jealous!

KATIE. I guess.

AMANDA. She is!

KATIE. I just — She thinks because she did that stupid pageant that she is better than everyone else and she's not!

AMANDA. Yeah, but we are gonna prove her so wrong! *(Amanda checks her text messages.)* Hey! Speaking of… Aaaahhhhh!!!!!

KATIE. What?

AMANDA. Nothing. Nothing that concerns you.

KATIE. What!?

AMANDA. Nothing. Hey Amber —

KATIE. Hey — *(The girls wave.)*

AMANDA. Call me about Bible study on Wednesday. My dad can totally give you a ride. *(The girls watch her walk by. After a moment.)*

KATIE. Why do you talk to her?

AMANDA. She's a nice person. Plus, Jesus wants me to be nice to the less fortunate. You should know that of all people!

KATIE. She's in *Special Ed*. You'll never be popular if you talk to her. So? Tell me!

AMANDA. Nothing.

KATIE. *Mandy* come on!

AMANDA. Don't call me Mandy! My name is not Mandy it is Amanda and if you call me that one more time I'm gonna punch you in the face! Josh just sent me THE text message!

KATIE. Are you serious? Ohmigosh are you serious? He got them?

AMANDA. Shhh… He's gonna give us a ride to my house after school.

KATIE. I can't believe he got them! Pixie Chicks!

AMANDA. Shut up! Mr. Branbalt is like right behind you! He is so creepy. *(They watch Mr. Branbalt walk by.)* Didn't I tell you Josh would come through, but you never listen to a word I say! *(Katie stuffs food into her mouth and opens it to gross out Amanda.)*

KATIE. You wanna make out with me!

AMANDA. What is wrong with you? I hope Rob sees you like that! Relax.

KATIE. I am relaxed! I just — this is the first time in my life something remotely exciting has happened! I can't wait to get out of this school and do something meaningful for once in our lives! Oh, oh, oh, oh, oh, oh so how do you think you did on the math test?

AMANDA. I think I did pretty good. I was up all night studying stupid common denominators… Seriously, I didn't go to bed till like three in the morning and I didn't even have time to practice our routine and I could barely sleep… I just — I'm really nervous! My parents will kill me if I get a bad grade!

KATIE. I know! Last time I got an A minus. An A minus! I studied so long for that stupid test and she gives me an A minus! I bet she can't even do half the problems on that test. She just has her little teacher book with all her little teacher answers. An A minus! I was so pissed —

AMANDA. God!

KATIE. Amanda!

AMANDA. What?

KATIE. Don't use the Lord's name in vain! It is very un–Christian of you.

AMANDA. My bad. Gosh! I am so happy we are finally done with Mrs. Jeffers! She is so ignorant! I am so sick of ignorant people acting like they know what is going on all the time!

KATIE. That old, wrinkled psycho! I swear she is lucky today is the last day of school because if I had to look at her rat eyes one more time I might jab them out with my pencil. And she is so mean to me and she always looks at me funny and I bet that's why she gave me an A minus! I bet it is my boobs.

AMANDA. No it isn't! She looks at everyone funny. Josh told me the teachers in high school are so much nicer and laid back and they don't even care what you do. He said that most teachers want to teach high school because the students there are so much more mature and all the crappy teachers get stuck in middle school.

KATIE. I hope so.

AMANDA. Well Josh would know. He is a Junior!

KATIE. I know! I wasn't questioning him so relax! Gosh, I can't believe you still haven't tried to make out with him —

AMANDA. Shut up! I'm not a slut! I'm saving myself like Pastor Jim says.

KATIE. Yeah, but he's always at your house mowing your lawn without his shirt on!

AMANDA. So?

KATIE. I would totally do it with him! And he got us the "you-know-whats" so technically you owe him something—

AMANDA. Why is Zach sitting by Erica? I thought they broke up!

KATIE. They did. But then they got back together during first period.

AMANDA. Oh my gosh…

KATIE. What?

AMANDA. I just realized this is our last lunch in this cafeteria. This is our last lunch in middle school. This is our last lunch as girls. Do you realize that? This is like such a huge moment in our lives. As soon as the bell rings after fourth period we're high school women! I have to tape this! *(Amanda pulls out her camera.)*

KATIE. Amanda, this is stupid! You can't carry that thing everywhere we go!

AMANDA. Yes I can! I'm gonna make a documentary of our lives and put it on Facebook and MySpace and Youtube! *(Katie reaches over and turns the camera off.)* HEY slut—

KATIE. You can't tape everything we do.

AMANDA. Yes I can.

KATIE. Look at me. You can't tape everything we do. Got it?

AMANDA. Oh… I didn't think about that. I'm retarded. *(A school bell rings.)*

Scene Three

Amanda is in the hallway cleaning her locker as Katie enters.

AMANDA. Remember this picture?

KATIE. Ohmigosh yeah! Wow we look so young and that was only last year! Amanda, I don't know if I want to do this… We could get in so much trouble for the fake I.D.s—

AMANDA. Shut up! There are teachers around, Katie!

KATIE. My mother would ground me for the entire summer if she knew I spent my allowance on that! And she would tell your mom and your mom would ground you and then everything would be ruined and our friendship would be over because if I had to look at you after you destroyed my summer I would be forced to murder you!

AMANDA. OK, OK, God you are so fucking dramatic!

KATIE. What is with your mouth today?

AMANDA. What? We're gonna be in high school. We have to talk like we are women now, not children.

KATIE. So you have to say the F-word?

AMANDA. It is a form of self-expression. What? They say it on HBO all the time and you never complain about that. Cover your virgin ears if you don't like it.

KATIE. Yeah, but there is a huge difference between TV language and language good Christian girls use. I doubt any of the people on HBO go to church every Sunday, Amanda. God put them here for our entertainment and nothing more. They definitely aren't going to Heaven. Speaking of self-expression, did you see what Kylie wore today? I think she is just trying to get Rob's attention! She looked like a total slut walking around school in that tiny skirt and all that makeup! That really pisses me off! He is way too good for her!

AMANDA. Yeah gross! She looked like some Britney wanna-be! *(Amanda sings a Britney Spears song at the top of her voice and starts to do their dance routine. Katie stops her in shock and embarrassment. They watch as Kylie and the popular girls walk toward them.)* I bet she's not wearing any panties! I mean you can practically see her ass! I don't understand girls like that! I mean, it's enough that she brags about that stupid pageant all the time and now she has to dress like —

KATIE. Kylie is looking over here! I think she knows we're talking about her —

AMANDA. I don't care. *(They watch the popular girls walk by.)*

KATIE. Those girls have no self-respect. I bet if our parents let us do that pageant we so would have won. Besides, Rob totally wants me not Kylie. He is soooooo hot...

AMANDA. Maybe if you start hanging out with Kylie and all the popular girls he would notice you. Speaking of the Evil Ones, Dana told me that she heard Kerry and Gina talking to Trisha who heard Erica and Lynn talking to Angela who heard Sarah and Justine talking to Jennifer in the locker room talking about how Kylie and Vanessa are having S-E-X with high school guys—

KATIE. No way!

AMANDA. Yeah! Kylie and Vanessa gave a blowjob to two guys on the soccer team at the same time!

KATIE. Blowjobs aren't S-E-X! S-E-X is only S-E-X if it goes in!

AMANDA. Let's go ask Pastor Jim if giving a blowjob is S-E-X or not!

KATIE. No way! Pastor Jim would have a coronary! Plus he doesn't know about stuff like that!

AMANDA. Let's ask your dad!

KATIE. Gross! My dad would have a coronary! *(They see Kylie walk by.)*

AMANDA. Someday when we're rich and famous and on the cover of every magazine everyone who was ever mean to us will hate themselves for it.

KATIE. I can't wait.

AMANDA. I'm so nervous.

KATIE. About tonight?

AMANDA. I'm afraid I'll forget our routine…

KATIE. No one can find out about this ever! Ever!

AMANDA. I know! Pinky swear with spit! *(Both girls spit on their pinkies and latch them together. The sound of students rushing through hallways is heard.)*

Scene Four

It is the last period. The girls are sitting next to each other. They are pretending like they are taking notes as Mr. Branbalt drones on in a monotonous voice in the background.

AMANDA. We're not going to get caught.

KATIE. I'm just saying…

AMANDA. We're at Dana's place for Bible study sleepover. And I told Dana we were seeing the Blink 182 concert and that I'd try to get her an autograph! You know how obsessed she is with them! Dana will totally cover for us!

KATIE. What if she doesn't?

AMANDA. Stop freaking out!

KATIE. I'm not freaking out!

AMANDA. Yes you are!

KATIE. No I'm not!

AMANDA. Yes you are!

KATIE. No I'm not!

MR. BRANBALT (VO). I know this is the last day of middle school, Amanda and Katie, but please hold your personal conversations until the bell rings.

AMANDA. Sorry, Mr. Branbalt. *(Overlapping.)*

KATIE. Sorry, Mr. Branbalt. *(A few moments pass as they pretend to be paying attention.)* Believe what you want.

AMANDA. I hope they don't think I'm fat.

KATIE. You're not fat. No one thinks you're fat.

AMANDA. Vanessa and Kylie told me I was fat in gym class. They said I should invest in diet pills and a gym membership over the summer, then Vanessa said I should just stop eating.

KATIE. Let me see the ad. *(Amanda pulls out a piece of crumpled paper printed from the internet and hands it to Katie.)* "Hollywood Talent Scout Looking for New Faces!" Kylie's dumb pageant didn't have a Hollywood talent scout! We are gonna be so famous and then you can get liposuction if you want. *(Amanda punches Katie in the arm and both girls begin to giggle.)*

MR. BRANBALT (VO). What's so funny ladies? *(Overlapping.)*

AMANDA. Nothing, Mr. Branbalt.

KATIE. Nothing, Mr. Branbalt.

MR. BRANBALT (VO). Would you like to share with the rest of the class? *(Overlapping.)*

AMANDA. No, Mr. Branbalt!

KATIE. No, Mr. Branbalt!

MR. BRANBALT (VO). What's in your hand, Katie? *(Both girls are horrified.)*

KATIE. Just a funny cartoon.

MR. BRANBALT (VO). Bring it to the front of the class and share with everyone. *(Amanda shakes her head no. Both girls fidget uncomfortably. Overlapping.)*

AMANDA. She'll put it away right now! We didn't mean it!

KATIE. I'm really sorry and I will put it away. *(Katie tries to put the paper in her notebook.)*

MR. BRANBALT (VO). Well now, the whole class is curious and we'd all like a good laugh at a funny cartoon. Please bring that to me. *(Katie slowly starts to rise and walk toward the front of the class. Amanda starts to hyperventilate. Suddenly the bell rings. There is a commotion from all the other kids as they celebrate the end of middle school. Amanda leaps out of her desk, grabs her and Katie's notebooks and Katie's arm and runs toward the door.)*

AMANDA. Sorry, Mr. Branbalt, but you can't make us because we're in high school now!

Youth Group Lesson Two

Flashback. Pastor Jim resumes his place in the middle of the stage.

PASTOR JIM. There is only ONE answer. Only one real, true answer. It is Jesus Christ our Lord and Savior. Jesus must really be in your heart to get to Heaven! And you can't fool God. You can fool yourself and your friends and your parents and even me, but you can't fool God. Who thinks they have Jesus in their hearts? Raise your hands. Oooohhhhh, interesting. Almost everyone is raising their hand. Wow, well I guess my job here is done. Cool. Well I'm gonna go play some golf. *(The voices of protesting kids fill the room.)* Interesting… I guess you guys aren't so sure. And if you're not so sure, then that means God knows you don't really have Jesus in your heart. But before we can truly accept Jesus we have to cleanse ourselves of sin. How many of you have sinned recently? Think about it, guys... Think about it really hard... Told a lie, thought about S-E-X, looked at inappropriate pictures on the internet or saw an R rated movie, played a violent video game or watched MTV or HBO? Just think about it, guys. You don't have to answer me, but I want you to think about all those yucky feelings that happen when you commit a sin. How does that make you feel inside? Dirty? Guilty? Ashamed? That is what sin does to you. Even the smallest sin. Once upon a time, I was about your age, if you guys can believe that. No snickering, Rob. One day I went into this convenience store to buy a Snickers, because I still believe that Snickers bars are the greatest food in the world. There was this little old lady in front of me buying some milk. She handed the cashier a twenty and he handed her back her change. She reached for the milk, and she dropped a dollar and didn't see it. So I picked it up and used it to pay for my candy. I thought it was no big deal. I ate the candy and went on with my day. That night I had a horrible nightmare about snakes and fire and a car crash. It happened night after night after night and I had no idea why. It was so bad that I couldn't sleep anymore so I went to my older brother Todd. He asked me if I had done anything wrong. That's when I realized I had stolen that lady's dollar. It was a small sin, but it haunted me. So Todd and I prayed for Jesus to enter my heart and forgive me from weakness. That night the nightmares stopped. So what do you think, guys? If we died right now would any of us go to Heaven? No. Not a single one of us. How scary is that? How can any of us sleep at night? How can any of us look in the mirror?

Video Montage Three — Amanda's Bedroom

Amanda has the camera set up so that you can see the back of her and Katie as they do their hair and makeup in the mirror. We never see their faces. They are listening to loud music. Katie doesn't realize the camera is on.

AMANDA. Hurry up! We have to leave before my parents come home and see us! My mom says I can't wear makeup till I'm sixteen!

KATIE. We should practice one more time before we go.

AMANDA. OK, but fast! *(Katie goes to change the song they are listening to. She notices the camera.)*

KATIE. Why is the red light flashing? Are you recording this? What is wrong with you? I told you not to record ANY of this! *(Katie turns the camera off.)*

On the Bus

All we see is the ceiling of the bus. We only hear their conversation. The camera is turned on sticking through a hole in Amanda's backpack. Katie is not aware of this.

AMANDA. Our big adventure begins! I am so excited!

KATIE. You can see the lights of the city from here!

AMANDA. This is crazy! Ohmigosh, I am so excited! There are a lot of weird people on this bus. That old guy in the corner smells really bad!

KATIE. So funny! Shhh... *(The sound of hydraulic brakes creak. END OF VIDEO MONTAGE.)*

Scene Five

In the darkness we hear pounding drums getting louder and faster. Lights begin to flash, red, green, blue, purple. The drums and lights become more and more intense. Then we hear a strip club DJ.

DJ (VO). Welcome to the Claaaasssssy Mirrrraaaaage! Tonight is a very special night, in fact it is our favorite night here at the Classy Mirage! Amateur night! That's right gentlemen, you get to witness first hand some of the most beautiful, undiscovered flesh Iowa has to offer! We have fifteen gorgeous girls competing for your attention, gentlemen — make sure you show them some love, guys! If you want to see those sexy bodies again and again and again toss them a few dollars so we can keep them coming back! Tonight's grand prize is five hundred dollars and an audition with Hollywood Talent Vixen Company! Kicking the night off we have the amazing, the incredible, the incredibly sexxxxy Gloria! *(Lights up on a cramped, filthy bathroom. Music plays in the background. Katie and Amanda scamper in. They are half-dressed, wearing zip-up hoodies to hide their skimpy outfits. We see them without the retainer, glasses, headband and frumpy clothes for the first time. They continue getting ready in the mirror as they talk.)*

AMANDA. Ohmigod, ohmigod, ohmigod!

KATIE. I am so freaked out right now! Did you see how she was looking at us? She totally wanted to steal our routine!

AMANDA. She wanted to see you take your clothes off!

KATIE. No way! You think she's a lesbo? Pastor Jim says that is one of the worst sins anyone can commit!

AMANDA. Ewwww!

KATIE. I'm so scared! I've never been around a lesbian before!

AMANDA. Katie! That's so mean! You shouldn't say things like that about people you don't know!

KATIE. Then you go back out there and change in front of her!

AMANDA. No way!

KATIE. Then don't get mad at me for saying she's a lesbo! You know all gays have AIDS!

AMANDA. Shut up! What if she hears you and she comes in here and tries to be a lesbo with us and we get AIDS?

KATIE. What if we already have it?

AMANDA. Shut up! *(Suddenly there is pounding on the door.)*

KATIE. Aaahhhh!

AMANDA. Ohmigod, ohmigod, ohmigod —

IRATE STRIPPER (VO). I have to pee so hurry the fuck up! *(After a moment.)*

KATIE. I don't think we should be doing this.

AMANDA. You wanna chicken out on me? Do you?

KATIE. No... I didn't say that...

AMANDA. We are in this together. There is a Hollywood talent scout out there and this could be the only chance we ever get our whole lives to really do something and get out of this place!

KATIE. I don't want to take my clothes off...

AMANDA. We don't have to. We just have to dance really good. That's why he is here. To judge who the best dancers are so they can be in movies.

KATIE. I don't know…

AMANDA. This is how I look at it. We dance all the time, right? Right? In our bedrooms and ballet lessons when we were five and school dances. I mean at the last dance we had all the girls were wearing short skirts and tight shirts and just as much makeup as we are now. And you saw what Kylie wore to school? We're gonna try out for cheerleading in high school and they wear short skirts and kick their legs up in front of boys so everyone can see up their skirts. So what is the difference between dancing there and here or anywhere else for that matter? Nothing. This is what girls do. It is the way God made us. He is in control of all the circumstances in our lives and He brought us here so we should totally trust that Katie! I mean, if we didn't do this we would be totally *blasphamising* him! Besides, if we get famous then we can spread the word of Jesus Christ. And isn't that ultimately what Jesus says we should be doing?

KATIE. Of course.

AMANDA. So don't you think we owe it to Jesus and the plan God has for us to do this?

KATIE. Yes. All right, yes! I wish Rob were here.

AMANDA. Ohmigod will you shut up about Rob for like five seconds?

KATIE. I didn't even say anything.

IRATE STRIPPER (VO). Hurry the fuck up!

KATIE. Sorry! We're almost done! *(Both girls pull off their hoodies revealing very skimpy, matching outfits that they have decorated with glitter glue. "Pixie Chicks" is written across the chest.)*

AMANDA. You look like a *Playboy* model!

KATIE. Really?

AMANDA. I wish I had big boobs! If I don't get big boobs by tenth grade, I am saving up for a boob job. I want them this big, then I will shake them in your face! *(Amanda shakes her chest in Katie's face.)*

KATIE. Ohmigosh, get those mosquito bites out of my face before I bite them off! Amanda?

AMANDA. Yeah?

KATIE. I'm glad we are in this together.

AMANDA. Me too.

KATIE. Practice? *(The girls begin to practice their routine. Suddenly they are interrupted when the DJ comes on over the speaker.)*

DJ (VO). Wow! Wow! Wasn't she amazing! They don't get much hotter than that, boys! Sexxxy! And she says she is only nineteen! Can't be nineteen with knockers like that! Am I right guys? I am completely out of breath! All right, all right, what do we have next? I have a very special treat for you, gentlemen. Get ready to feast your eyes on this amazing duo. You heard me right! There are two of them. The Pixie Chicks! *(Music with intense drums, almost like a heartbeat, plays.)*

KATIE. This is just between you and me right? *(Overlapping.)*

AMANDA. I've got Jesus! Yes I do! I've got Jesus! How 'bout you?

KATIE. I've got Jesus! Yes I do! I've got Jesus! How 'bout you? *(They spit on their pinkies and latch them together then head to the stage.)*

Scene Six

The girls enter the stage. The lights are bright and there are cheers from men. They stand there frozen for a moment. Then they count to themselves and begin their routine. Their movements are stiff and awkward, more like something you would see at a school talent show than at a strip club. After a few minutes of dancing and no stripping, the crowd begins to boo them. Katie stops dancing and is on the verge of tears. Amanda starts to dance more seductively, but still very childlike. Katie joins in. The more sexual they become, the louder the crowd cheers until someone yells for them to take off their clothes. Both girls freeze. Katie looks at Amanda and shakes her head "no." Amanda hesitates going back and forth between the chanting crowd and Katie's face. After a moment, Amanda starts to undo her top as she looks at Katie. Katie shakes her head "no" again. The crowd cheers louder for Amanda to continue. She pulls off her top revealing her breasts. Katie is shocked. The men cheer. Katie runs off stage. Amanda continues dancing. BLACK OUT.

Video Montage Four

More images of celebrities in skimpy outfits flash across the screen.

A Diner

The girls and Frank at a local diner. Katie is quiet in the corner. It is obvious she is nervous and doesn't want to be there. Amanda is excited. She has the camera turned on sitting on her lap. Frank and Katie are not aware of this. We see Frank and Katie's legs and body language, but never their faces. We only hear their conversation.

AMANDA. So even though Katie ruined the dance competition, you still think we have a chance?

FRANK. That's right. As long as you ladies have a good screen test.

KATIE. A what?

FRANK. A screen test. Hollywood protocol. I have everything set up. And if my bosses, who are big producers, like you girls… The sky is the limit. You girls are eighteen right? I mean you look so young it freaks me out a little… But that's what people love.

AMANDA. We are. Ooohhh! Wanna see our I.D.s?

FRANK. If you want to show them to me. *(Amanda fumbles around in the backpack accidentally turning the camera off.)*

Frank's Car

Frank is driving. The girls are in the back seat. They are all singing at the top of their lungs. We never see Frank's face. END OF VIDEO MONTAGE.

Youth Group Lesson Three

Flashback. Pastor Jim stands in the center of the stage.

PASTOR JIM. I've always been honest with you guys, right? You know I'm not perfect. I've made a lot of mistakes that I can never take back. We all have. That's life and that's growing up. And now that you guys are almost grown-up I want to share with you something very personal. Something that made me… Made me know that I must devote myself to saving as many souls as I can in this lifetime. *(He stands there in silence for several moments.)* I don't share this with a lot of people, so you guys are gonna have to bear with me… When I was in high school, I went to a party with my older brother Todd. Man, Todd was my idol. The way he dressed, the way he acted, the way girls looked at him, the way my parents respected him… He was everything I ever hoped to be. So when he invited me to this party, which he never did, it was a huge deal! I was sixteen. Todd was nineteen. I put on my best clothes, my best shoes, combed my hair just like him. We got to this party and there was a ton of booze and pot. And Todd did all of it. The guy I admired most in the world. The guy that taught me to shave. And here he was doing something I thought he'd *never* touch. He offered me some and I did it. I wanted to impress him. I wanted him to love me and think I was fun to hang with. I drank till I was almost puking. I smoked a joint. And then the flashing lights of cop cars appeared outside. Todd was passed out. So I dragged him to the car before he would get in trouble. His girlfriend and her best friend climbed in the back seat. I was so messed up guys… *(He pauses for a moment, trying to keep control of his emotions.)* I climbed in the driver's seat. And this, this force came over me. Like it crawled inside of me and took over my body. I thought I was invincible. Just like when I was a kid wandering through that cave. I revved up the engine just as a cop, with a hand on his gun belt, knocked on the window. So what did I do? I took off going a hundred and two miles per hour down a suburban street. I tried to make a sharp turn, but lost control and the car flew into a telephone pole with such force that the pole splintered and flew through the windshield impaling Todd in the head. The back end of the car wrapped around the stump of the pole still standing and crushed Todd's girlfriend and her friend. I didn't have a scratch. I thought it was a joke. I thought they had gotten fake blood and planned the whole thing. The cops pulled me out of the car and I was laughing hysterically. Of course, later I found out they were all dead before they even had a chance to open their eyes. They were all dead before they had a chance to ask Jesus into their hearts and souls. They were all dead before they had a chance to ask for forgiveness for all the sins they committed at that party… *(His eyes well with tears.)* My hero… My hero… My hero is spending eternity in that pitch-black cave because he never had the chance to ask for forgiveness. I was tried as an adult and spent three years in jail for manslaughter. I asked Jesus into my heart and begged for His forgiveness. And He forgave me, guys. I get a place in Heaven. And they get eternity in Hell. *(He wipes away his tears.)* We've got to acknowledge our sins, guys. And we can't say maybe later or maybe tomorrow. We've got to do it now. It is far too important. Then we must ask Jesus to forgive us for all of our sins from the deepest parts of our heart and soul, and then we must accept Him as our one and only Savior. So I want everyone in the room to stand up. Stand up and stretch your arms high over your heads. Higher! Reach as high as you possibly can and try to touch God. He's watching you guys so touch him! Now everyone do jumping jacks. *(He does jumping jacks.)* Come on, Amanda and Katie! Stop giggling and passing notes. All right guys, now as we jump up and down I want everyone to shout out their sins! Everyone has a sin so no one should be silent! Everything from impure thoughts to video games or R rated movies to revealing clothes or inappropriate music or inappropriate use of the internet or alcohol or drugs or S-E-X! I won't judge you. No one will judge you in this room. *(The kids shout out their sins in a cacophony that is hard to decipher. They giggle from embarrassment.)*

KIDS (VO). I saw an R rated movie. I lied to my parents. I cheated on a test. I watched five hours of MTV and didn't do my homework. I lied to a teacher. I kissed my boyfriend. I wore red lipstick. I listened to Britney Spears. I looked at bad pictures online!

PASTOR JIM. LOUDER! FASTER!

KIDS (VO). I saw an R rated movie. I lied to my parents. I cheated on a test. I watched five hours of MTV and didn't do my homework. I lied to a teacher. I kissed my boyfriend. I wore red lipstick. I listened to Britney Spears. I looked at bad pictures online!

Scene Seven

A bus station. The girls sit on a bench waiting for their bus back to the suburbs. Amanda wipes the makeup off her face, and hands a small cloth to Katie so she can do the same. Then Amanda puts her glasses and headband back on and her retainer back in her mouth. She goes from adult to child in the blink of an eye. Amanda pulls out her cell phone. The silence is awkward.

AMANDA. I should call Dana.

KATIE. Did she call you?

AMANDA. No.

KATIE. Oh. *(Another long silence. Amanda dials her cell phone.)*

AMANDA. Hey… Sorry to wake you up. Did my parents or Katie's parents call? Oh yeah? Thanks, I owe you one. Yeah, yeah the concert was pretty cool. No... I couldn't get close enough to get an autograph... We're waiting for the bus back... I don't know, maybe an hour... Your parents aren't gonna freak when they see me and Katie? Oh yeah? Awesome. OK... Good-night.

KATIE. Did they call?

AMANDA. My mom called once to tell Dana to remind me to take my allergy pills. *(Silence.)* Dana left the back door open for us with the couch pulled out.

KATIE. That was nice of her.

AMANDA. She's a good friend.

KATIE. Yep.

AMANDA. Those cameras were pretty cool. I didn't realize how many you need for a professional screen test. And all the lights... Totally professional...

KATIE. Where's the stupid bus?

AMANDA. I don't know... Hey?

KATIE. What?

AMANDA. I dare you to go tie that homeless guy's shoes together. Do it. That would be so funny when he gets up! *(Katie giggles despite herself.)* I made you laugh!

KATIE. Shut up.

AMANDA. Sorry... Where is your sense of adventure?

KATIE. Sense of adventure? Are you out of your mind? Were you not there tonight? Were we not doing horrible disgusting things together tonight? I have never felt so degraded in my entire life! I don't know how I will ever be able to look myself in the mirror! I never thought I would hate you, Amanda, but right now I hate you more than anyone on the face of this planet! Because of you, I am going to Hell. Because of you, everything I have ever wanted in my whole life is ruined. Does every girl have to do that to become famous? I love our church. I love Pastor Jim. I love my parents. I pledged my virginity to Jesus Christ until I get married and now I don't know how I will ever look at myself in the mirror again! I don't know how I can ever go on a date with a decent boy ever again. I don't think any boy will ever want me now that I am ruined. Or Rob? How can I ever look at Rob again? I am a slut. I am nothing more than a slut. Thank you, Amanda. Just this afternoon I was a good Christian girl who was going to Heaven. And the one person I thought I could trust totally used me for nothing. I hate you. When we get home I want you to get all of your stuff out of my house and give me back everything I ever gave you including the autographed Jonas Brothers poster and the stuffed elephant from second grade and even the plastic mood ring! And I never ever want to see you again and don't call me ever again, and next year in high school you can find a new group of friends. I will ask Jesus for forgiveness and I will pray for you. I will pray that Jesus forgives us both. *(Silence.)*

AMANDA. Are you finished? *(No answer.)* Can I say something now? I'm sorry if you think I ruined your life tonight, Katie. And I'm sorry if you want to blame me for it and you never want to see me or be my bestest best friend again and that hurts me more than you will ever know because I would give my life for you. I'm the only one at school that sticks up for you when everyone talks behind your back and calls you ugly and fat and stupid. I'm the one that sticks up for you when Rob says he wouldn't touch you because he doesn't want herpes. But you obviously don't care about those things and I am just disposable like a piece of trash. And I don't want you to pray for me because I wouldn't want someone who hates me to pray for me. And how can I give you everything back? Do you want me to dig up Ralphie The Hamster that you gave me in third grade? And I don't even know where that stupid stuffed elephant is! But I just want to tell you something — Jesus loves us no matter what we do. He loves the whole world. John 3:16 Katie! John 3:16! Pastor Jim says that to us over and over and over again and everyone seems to understand that except for you because you are soooooo dramatic and your life is ruined when it isn't. I also think you have a very short memory because you wanted to do this as much as I did and you're the one that found the ad and picked out our costumes and got the glitter glue and you are the one who always talks about being a celebrity so you could have a big house and nice clothes and a horse and go on talk shows and spread the word of Jesus. This is what you wanted, Katie. And I, as your best friend, tried to give that to you any way that I could. And I thought that we had a good time tonight.

I thought we had the time of our lives. And we met a Hollywood talent scout and we did a real screen test and we may have gotten a little carried away, but I don't think we did anything wrong. And even if we did I know, I know deep deep in my heart that Jesus will forgive us. He knows my heart and he knows your heart. He knows we are good people. You and me, Katie and Amanda. We are good Christians. Now doesn't Pastor Jim always say Jesus will forgive all of our transgressions?

KATIE. Yes.

AMANDA. And if we have transgressed tonight, don't you think Jesus will forgive us?

KATIE. Yes.

AMANDA. Then I honestly don't know why you said all of those hateful things to me and why you are so willing to dump me as your best friend when we always promised each other we would be there no matter what. I really don't understand why you are being such a baby. And a bitch.

KATIE. Sorry.

AMANDA. Take back what you said.

KATIE. I take it back. I'm sorry. I love you, Amanda. *(They embrace tearfully.)* I'm so sorry, Amanda. I don't know why I said all those mean things to you. I love you!

AMANDA. I love you too!

KATIE. Please forgive me! You have to forgive me! I swear if you don't forgive me I will kill myself!

AMANDA. I forgive you.

KATIE. Thank you. I truly don't deserve a friend like you. *(After a moment.)* Should we ask Jesus to forgive us?

AMANDA. He already has. I already asked him and we are pure again.

KATIE. I feel better.

AMANDA. I keep seeing it in my head.

KATIE. What? Ewwwww! Don't think about it.

AMANDA. I can't believe that is what all the fuss is about.

KATIE. Me too. It wasn't even fun.

AMANDA. I don't even feel different. All the grown-ups say it changes you and makes you a different person, but I don't feel anything.

KATIE. He liked it way more than us that's for sure!

AMANDA. I couldn't get over the faces he made!

KATIE. He looked like he was in pain or something like this — *(Katie imitates Frank. Both girls giggle.)*

AMANDA. Ewwwww! Ohmigod!

KATIE. Amanda, you have to stop using the Lord's name in vain.

AMANDA. Sorry, Katie.

KATIE. Don't apologize to me. Apologize to God.

AMANDA. Sorry, God. Please forgive me for saying "God."

KATIE. That's better. Amanda…

AMANDA. Wanna go to the mall tomorrow and get new clothes?

KATIE. Yeah! Nice clothes! Better than anything Kylie and Vanessa have! Amanda?

AMANDA. Yeah?

KATIE. Do you really think we will be famous?

AMANDA. Frank said we have more talent than Lindsay Lohan and Miley Cyrus and Britney Spears combined. We are special and as soon as the Hollywood people see our screen test we will probably be in every movie. Otherwise, why would he have given us all that money and wanted us to sign those papers?

KATIE. But I don't ever want to do that stuff again… I mean, at least not until I get married… Amanda?

AMANDA. What?

KATIE. Does that make us prostitutes?

AMANDA. What?

KATIE. I mean… Since he gave us money and all… And the stuff we did…

AMANDA. No. It makes us real actresses. How many S-E-X scenes are in movies and on HBO and reality shows that are way worse than what we did?

KATIE. Right. We're actresses and we were acting in a hot love scene and we are totally good at it! *(Katie starts to fake an orgasm. Amanda giggles and then joins in. The girls are hysterical after a few moments.)* If I had known that was what it was all about, I would have marched right up to Rob and taken him in the bathroom and shown him what a real woman does.

AMANDA. Katie?

KATIE. Yeah?

AMANDA. We should thank God for giving us this opportunity.

KATIE. You're totally right. *(The girls fold their hands and pray in silence. We hear the sound of a bus pull in the station.)*

Youth Group Lesson Four

Flashback. Pastor Jim is winded from jumping jacks. Kids giggle. He smiles and under his breath says a little prayer to God.

PASTOR JIM. Luke 23:34, "Father, forgive them; for they know not what they do." *(END OF ACT ONE.)*

ACT II

In the darkness we hear a choir of children singing "Jesus Loves Me."

Video Montage One

Photos of celebrities in bikinis flash across the screen while the choir sings. BLACK OUT.

Scene One

The public pool. A month before high school begins. The girls are lying on pool chairs sunbathing. They wear bikinis and large sunglasses and heels. They are very Lolita-esque. Their hair is done and they wear makeup. Amanda no longer has the retainer and glasses. It is hard to believe that these are the same girls. Katie flips through a teen magazine as Amanda rubs sunscreen on her thighs. A whistle is heard.

AMANDA. So gross. I'm so tired of these dirty old men thinking they can have me. I'M TOO GOOD FOR YOU MR.!

KATIE. Amanda!

AMANDA. What?

KATIE. You made him cry. *(They giggle.)*

AMANDA. I was just thinking…

KATIE. What?

AMANDA. I can't wait to be on the cover of *Teen Vogue* and *Cosmo* and *US Weekly* all at the same time!

KATIE. Me too! I bet Kylie would be so jealous and Rob would totally dump her after he saw me!

AMANDA. I checked my phone like four times yesterday and I had a call from a blocked number and I am pretty sure it was Frank. He's probably waiting to call us until he has the whole movie deal worked out. That stuff takes awhile to negotiate. Ohmigod, ohmigod, ohmigod, I hope Zac Efron is in it!

KATIE. Amanda?

AMANDA. I mean I was reading in *Cosmo Girl* that when Miley Cyrus is negotiating movie deals it sometimes can take like six months because there is so much to cover. I feel so bad for Frank having to do that with two of us. We should totally give him twenty percent!

KATIE. Do you think I'm ugly?

AMANDA. It's just that if I have to be here through high school I will totally die! I already picked out my outfit for *The Late Show* and *The Tonight Show*. Ohmigod! We are going to have to do so much publicity once we get to Hollywood! Everyone is going to want us on their shows!

KATIE. Oh, oh, oh, oh, oh! I talked to Dana yesterday and she said she saw Rob and Kylie at the mall arguing and Rob got mad and stormed off! I bet he is starting to realize what a mistake he made with her… I totally have a shot with him in high school. I bet once I make the cheerleading squad —

AMANDA. Holy fuck! *(Overlapping.)*

KATIE. Don't swear! What?

AMANDA. Jesus, forgive me! So there! Fuck! Don't look, but Kylie, Vanessa and Rob just walked in —

KATIE. Ohmigosh! Kylie has gotten fat. She looks like a fat cow. I do not know why Rob wastes his time.

AMANDA. Should we talk to them?

KATIE. No. Don't even make eye contact. *(The girls go back to reading their magazines. Katie fixes her makeup. After a few moments.)*

AMANDA. Rob is totally drooling over you. *(Katie tries to play it cool.)*

KATIE. So?

AMANDA. So do something to make Kylie and Vanessa jealous.

KATIE. Like what?

AMANDA. I don't know.

KATIE. Think of something!

AMANDA. You are such a wuss! This is exactly why we lost the dance competition!

KATIE. That was mean, Amanda. You promised we would never talk about that —

AMANDA. Well, it's true. Rob is never going to want you because you are too much of a wuss to ever do anything.

KATIE. What should I do? Tell me.

AMANDA. OH MY GOD! I think he is French kissing Kylie. He doesn't even know you're alive. I bet Dana was lying about seeing them at the mall. They look soooooo happy together. *(Katie's face changes as she watches Rob and Kylie kiss.)*

KATIE. Dare me?

AMANDA. Double dare you with spit. *(Amanda spits on her pinky. She and Katie latch fingers.)*

KATIE. OK. Just remember you dared me. *(Katie stands up and pulls Amanda to her feet.)* HEY ROB! YOU SHOULD BE WITH A REAL WOMAN INSTEAD OF THOSE FAT COWS! *(Katie French kisses Amanda. The kiss is sexual and explosive like something out of a teen movie.)* NOW IMAGINE WHAT I COULD DO TO YOU. P.S. THEY ARE REAL. *(She flashes him her bare breasts. Amanda is shocked. And jealous.)*

AMANDA. You are crazy and everyone is staring at us and now they think I am a lesbo! I can't believe you did that!

KATIE. You dared me, Amanda.

AMANDA. Yeah, but my little brother is over there! Pastor Jim's son is over there! What if he tells my parents? There are little kids and people everywhere! I can't believe you! You are such a slut!

KATIE. What!?

AMANDA. How could you do that!?

KATIE. But *you* dared me.

AMANDA. I didn't dare you to act like a prostitute!

KATIE. But—

AMANDA. Imagine what Jesus thinks about you right now. *(Amanda grabs her things and storms off. Katie lies back down on the chair. After a moment she folds her hands.)*

KATIE. Jesus, please forgive me. Amen. *(Katie smiles to herself.)*

Youth Group Lesson Five

Flashback. Pastor Jim stands in the middle of the stage listening to the kids finish their song.

KIDS (VO). "Jesus loves me this I know. For the Bible tells me so. Little ones to him belong. They are weak, but he is strong. Yes Jesus loves me. Yes Jesus loves me. Yes Jesus loves me, for the Bible tells me so." *(Pastor Jim claps with joy.)*

PASTOR JIM. John 3:16: "For God so loved the world that he gave his one and only Son, that whoever believes in Him shall not perish but have eternal life." Amen. Amen. Amen. That was great, guys. All right, let's take a breather for a moment. Go to the bathroom, get some juice, eat a cookie... or seven. Be ready to go in five minutes. *(A cacophony of bustling children is heard. Amanda and Katie sheepishly enter from the audience. Katie wears oversized clothes and doesn't comb her hair. Amanda wears glasses, a retainer, and a pink Hello Kitty headband.)*

KATIE. Pastor Jim?

PASTOR JIM. Yes Katie?

KATIE. I'm sorry you lost your brother.

AMANDA. Me too.

PASTOR JIM. Thank you, girls.

KATIE. If there's anything we can ever do...

AMANDA. Yeah. Anything.

PASTOR JIM. You two will be the first to know.

AMANDA. Pastor Jim?

PASTOR JIM. Yes?

AMANDA. I think he went to Heaven. I mean, wouldn't God know that he was a good guy that made a mistake and he would have asked for forgiveness if he had the chance?

PASTOR JIM. I wish... But God lays down his law and if we wander from that, for even just a split second, our punishment is our responsibility and not God's.

KATIE. I never thought about it like that...

PASTOR JIM. I know. Most of us don't. All right, everyone come on back. If you stuff one more cookie in your mouth Kylie will be so impressed with you, Rob! You girls want to be my helpers? *(Amanda and Katie nod. Katie watches Rob in awe.)* I want everyone to stand up. Amanda and Katie are going to stay up here on the stage with me and be my helpers. We are going to ask Jesus to forgive us for all of our sins right here and right now. Because today, these moments, could very well be our last. We could die in a car wreck or choke on our dinner or slip in the shower or some rare disease could take us while we sleep tonight. And I could not live with myself if any of you in this room didn't get to go to Heaven. So I want you all to shout out for forgiveness at the top of your lungs from the deepest parts of your heart. Please forgive me, Jesus! *(The voices of fellow children are heard along with Amanda and Katie. Overlapping.)*

AMANDA. Please forgive me, Jesus!

KATIE. Please forgive me, Jesus!

PASTOR JIM. Please, please, please forgive me, Jesus! *(Overlapping.)*

AMANDA. Please forgive me, Jesus!

KATIE. Please forgive me, Jesus!

PASTOR JIM. PLEASE, PLEASE, PLEASE, PLEASE FORGIVE ME, JESUS! PLEASE! *(The sound of children sniffling and crying is heard. Amanda and Katie hug each other as they fight back tears.)*

Video Montage Two

Shots of celebrities in unflattering states flash on the screen. Amanda's bedroom. She turns the camera on as she gives a monologue. She no longer has the retainer and Hello Kitty headband. She wears red lipstick.

AMANDA. Is it on? Hello? Are you on? Oh, OK. So welcome to my boring life. Let's see what has happened… High school starts in a few days and I am really nervous. My mom took me shopping for a bunch of new clothes so that is exciting. I got four Abercrombie shirts, a purple dress from Wet Seal, a yellow dress from Old Navy, three pairs of jeans from the Gap, and some stuff from Target including a backpack with red and white flowers. There will be a bunch of people from three other middle schools so I hope there will be a lot of cute boys… I haven't really talked to Katie since Rob became her boyfriend. She called me a few weeks ago, but other than that… I don't know. I miss her, but she is so different now. She's mean. Like at church a week ago she told this girl Amber not to come near her because she is a retard. Amber is a really nice girl and it isn't her fault she is in Special Ed… It's weird not having a best friend around, but I'm not Rob so I guess I'm not good enough. Dana told me that Katie has been spending the night at Kylie's and Vanessa's houses. And they all triple date because Kylie and Vanessa are dating some high school guys or something… But it doesn't matter because as soon as I get to Hollywood and become famous I won't even remember

Katie and she will regret how she treated me. I had this crazy dream the other night that I can't get out of my head. I am walking down the street in this really pretty blue dress and my hair and makeup are perfect and it is me, but it isn't me. Then this big Hollywood producer comes up to me and he tells me that I am just the girl he has been searching for. He tells me I am special and there is no other girl like me and I am meant to do great things. He tells me that I will be a BIG STAR. He tells me that is what God wants for me and I just have to have faith. And then I woke up and I had this calm feeling, ya know… Like the dream was a sign from God to just trust His plan. Like it is my destiny to be famous. Every day I sit by the phone and wait to hear from Frank or somebody in Hollywood. Anybody… *(END OF VIDEO MONTAGE.)*

Scene Two

Lights up on Amanda's bedroom. She bursts through the door hysterical. She tears apart her bag searching for her cell phone then frantically calls Katie. She no longer has the retainer and Hello Kitty headband. She wears red lipstick.

AMANDA. Hey… I know, but… Where are you? Come over! I don't care if you are with Rob! I don't care Katie! You have to come over right now! You live a block away, Katie, so tell Rob to entertain himself and run over here! You better be here in two minutes and I am timing you! Please, Katie, I am begging you! *(Amanda hangs up and throws the phone into the wall. She grabs a stuffed elephant and her Bible. Then she falls on the bed hysterical. After a few moments of sobbing she begins to pray.)* Dear God, please don't let my life be ruined! Please! I swear I will be good, just please don't let my life be ruined! Please! I will do whatever you want… I will be a good Christian girl and I will never sin again… Please God… *(Amanda closes her eyes and flips through the pages of the Bible. She blindly picks a passage, and then opens her eyes.)* "The LORD is near to all who call on Him, to all who call on Him in truth. He fulfills the desires of those who fear him; he hears their cry and saves them…" *(A moment later Katie enters in a huff. Katie wears makeup and tight clothes. Her hair is styled.)*

KATIE. What? What? What?

AMANDA. The screen test! Our screen test with Frank! It is on the internet!

KATIE. What!?

AMANDA. It is on the internet!

KATIE. How do you know?

AMANDA. My dad found it —

KATIE. How!?

AMANDA. I have no idea! He just called me from work and said he saw a video and —

KATIE. But —

AMANDA. It is on the internet and now my dad wants to go to the cops! He wants Frank arrested for child molestation!

KATIE. What!? How did he find the tape in the first place?

AMANDA. I have no idea! Do you know what this means? We are totally ruining any shot at being in movies if Frank gets in trouble! What happens if they find out in Hollywood that we are snitches?

KATIE. That's all you ever care about is Hollywood and you aren't even there!

AMANDA. I will be and you and everyone else are just jealous —

KATIE. No I'm not! I don't care about that stuff anymore. It is just a silly dream that is ruining my REAL life!

AMANDA. You don't know what you are talking about —

KATIE. Yes I do —

AMANDA. What do we do? He's gonna call your parents after my mom comes home and he tells her. What do we do?

KATIE. He can't tell my parents! I'm a virgin! My dad will hate me and I will never get to see Rob!

AMANDA. But you aren't a virgin —

KATIE. Yes I am —

AMANDA. I was there! You can't lie to me. I know what you did with Frank. And I heard what you've done with Rob.

KATIE. I've never done anything with Rob! He is a pure Christian boy, way more pure than you'll ever be! You take that back!

AMANDA. NO!

KATIE. I hate you! This is all your fault! I hate you!

AMANDA. Like you're so innocent! Shut up, Katie!

KATIE. I HATE YOU!!!! *(Amanda throws the stuffed elephant at Katie.)*

AMANDA. SHUT UP YOU STUPID SLUT!! You are nothing but a little slut that Jesus hates! You had *sex* with Frank and now it is all over the internet for the world to see and I bet Rob will dump you once he finds out what a slut you are!

KATIE. You will never get out of this town! YOU WILL NEVER BE FAMOUS BECAUSE YOU ARE JUST AN ORDINARY GIRL LIKE ME AND KYLIE AND VANESSA AND DANA AND EVERY OTHER GIRL IN THE WORLD! *(Amanda slaps Katie hard across the face. Katie is stunned.)*

AMANDA. I am not ordinary and I will NEVER be an ordinary slut like you. *(Katie hits Amanda back. Amanda pulls Katie's hair. Suddenly they are both screaming and rolling around on the floor fighting.)*

KATIE. I HATE YOU AND I WANT YOU TO DIE!

AMANDA. I HATE YOU!!! I HATE YOU!!! I HATE YOU!!! *(Ad-lib threats and insults for a few moments. Amanda spits in Katie's face. Suddenly both girls start to cry hysterically and hug each other. A few moments pass.)* Why did you ditch me for a boy? You promised you would always be my best friend...

KATIE. You've never been my friend. You just used me because no one else listened to you.

AMANDA. I never used you. I love you and I just wanted to give you a better life by making you famous. I just wanted you to be happy.

KATIE. I am happy. For the first time in my whole life I am really happy. You always made it seem like you can only be happy if you are a movie star so I believed that was what I wanted, but I'm not a movie star and I'm happy. I don't even want to be a movie star... I want to be a veterinarian who occasionally goes to see movies. What happened with Frank was horrible and I never want to do that ever again.

AMANDA. You're so delusional. You're just infatuated with a dumb boy who will probably break your heart and when that happens I will be in

Hollywood and no one will be here to pick up the pieces and be your best friend again. And you better believe that I am going to tell Frank that you are out of the picture and you will lose all the movie deals—

KATIE. I don't want movie deals anymore!

AMANDA. Yes you do. Everyone does! Everyone wants movie deals and nice clothes and big houses and tons of money and magazine covers and lots of attention! Because that is what makes people special in this world! And I will tell Frank that you went to the police and accused him of horrible things he didn't do and that I stuck up for him the whole time!

KATIE. He did do horrible things to us—

AMANDA. No he didn't, Katie. And I will stick up for him no matter what you or my dad or anyone else says.

KATIE. I'm not going to lose Rob.

AMANDA. Well I'm not going to lose my dream.

KATIE. I hope you burn in Hell! *(Katie picks up the stuffed elephant.)* And I'm taking this back! *(Katie storms out. Amanda pulls out a secret box from under her bed with "Our Big Break" written in glitter glue. She opens it and dumps the contents on the floor. The dance competition ad, her costume, and the tapes of that night. She smashes the tapes into tiny pieces, tears up the ad and shreds the costume with scissors.)*

AMANDA. Jesus loves you, Frank. And he forgives you. I asked him to forgive you.

Youth Group Lesson Six

Flashback. Pastor Jim sits on the stage with a tissue in his hand. The sniffles of kids are heard. He smiles at them.

PASTOR JIM. Now nobody laugh at me. I have a secret confession. My all-time favorite TV show is *Star Trek*. Zooming all over the universe in a space ship, cool gadgets, discovering exotic worlds and creatures… And the universe is so big that you could spend your whole life discovering new things and you'd only touch the tip of the iceberg. I imagine that Heaven is just like that only infinite and filled with God's love. New discoveries and beauties at every turn. Magical sunsets and beaches and warm oceans. And you're never lonely or sad or angry or hurt. Just overwhelming joy because God's love is everywhere. All we have to do is just endure the hurt and pain and sadness and loneliness in this lifetime and keep Jesus in our hearts and we get to spend eternity in a paradise far more amazing than even *Star Trek* adventures. And you guys are almost there. After these moments, your places in Heaven will be secured. *(Amanda and Katie scamper down through the audience with an empty box of tissues. Their eyes are red and they each clutch a used tissue. Katie wears oversized clothes and doesn't comb her hair. Amanda wears glasses, a retainer, and a pink Hello Kitty headband. Katie hands the empty box to Pastor Jim.)* Wow! You guys sure didn't go easy on the box of tissues. How we holding up, my helpers? *(The girls nod and smile.)* Today is the most important day of your lives. Today you guys are going to make a very sacred promise to God. Today each and every one of you will secure your place in Heaven. Repeat after me. "I promise you, God, in the name of your Only Son, that I will live a pure life." *(The voices of children are heard along with Amanda and Katie. Overlapping.)*

AMANDA. "I promise you, God, in the name of your Only Son, that I will live a pure life."

KATIE. "I promise you, God, in the name of your Only Son, that I will live a pure life."

PASTOR JIM. "I will fight to avoid temptation. And if I fall short I will ask for your forgiveness."

AMANDA. "I will fight to avoid temptation. And if I fall short I will ask for your forgiveness."

KATIE. "I will fight to avoid temptation. And if I fall short I will ask for your forgiveness."

PASTOR JIM. "And above all else, I will do everything in my power to spread the word of Jesus Christ so everyone has a chance at Heaven."

AMANDA. "And above all else, I will do everything in my power to spread the word of Jesus Christ so everyone has a chance at Heaven."

KATIE. "And above all else, I will do everything in my power to spread the word of Jesus Christ so everyone has a chance at Heaven."

PASTOR JIM. Amen. *(The sounds of kids' voices are heard. They are happy and free. Pastor Jim hugs Amanda and Katie.)*

Video Montage Three

Dramatic theme music to a talk show is heard in the darkness. A bright red "Applause" sign flashes.

Dr. Opal Banks Show

Two years have passed. A well-dressed woman, holding a microphone, DR. OPAL BANKS, 50, talks into the camera.

DR. OPAL BANKS. We are going to start today's show with the two young girls from Iowa who made national headlines when they were tricked into doing a dance contest, brutally raped, and then exploited on the internet for a profit. The monster that did this to them, Jim Grimes, A.K.A. Frank Miller, just received twenty-five years in prison for his horrific crime. He preyed upon every young girl's dream of stardom. The girls will be joining us from the steps of their church in Iowa, as their parents didn't think it fit for them to travel to our studios in Los Angeles. Please give a warm welcome to Katie and Amanda. *(The sign flashes as the lights come up on stage.)*

Scene Three

Video/Live Action. Amanda and Katie are in perfect dresses with their hair and makeup done. They look very mature and grown up. They both wear large buttons with the name of their church, God's Honor Chapel, pinned to their clothes. Bright lights surround them, almost drowning them. They both have an earpiece and a small microphone on their clothes. Katie fidgets nervously and is very quiet and reserved while Amanda panders to the camera the whole time. The girls hate each other and the tension between them could be cut with a knife. Throughout the scene they interact with Dr. Opal Banks who is seen ONLY on the monitor.

DR. OPAL BANKS. Katie? Amanda?

AMANDA. Yes?

KATIE. Yes?

DR. OPAL BANKS. Hello girls. Thank you for joining me. First of all, I want to tell you girls that I think you are very brave for coming on national television to tell your story. This is something that all young girls and parents need to hear.

AMANDA. Thank you for having us.

DR. OPAL BANKS. Let's get right to it. So the two of you found an ad for a "dance" competition?

AMANDA. Yes, Dr. Opal. We thought it was like *Dancing with the Stars* or *American Idol* or something like that. So we practiced our routine for weeks. And we made matching costumes and everything.

DR. OPAL BANKS. And then you show up to this seedy strip club?

AMANDA. Yes ma'am.

DR. OPAL BANKS. Why didn't you leave? You girls are smart enough to know that couldn't have been a legitimate competition.

AMANDA. I know that now, but I was only fourteen then and Katie and I had no clue. I'm sixteen now and I know so much more about the world. Plus, we went in through the back so we never saw what women were doing on the stage until we got on it.

DR. OPAL BANKS. And what happened?

AMANDA. It's such a blur. I have so much trouble remembering… The doctors say that "dissociative amnesia" is normal in traumatic events…

DR. OPAL BANKS. Take your time, Amanda.

AMANDA. Thank you, Dr. Opal… *(Her eyes well with tears.)* Katie and I left. Katie ran off stage…

DR. OPAL BANKS. So how did you meet "Frank"?

AMANDA. Katie and I were walking out of the club and he came up to us and said he was the talent scout from Hollywood and he wanted us to do a screen test for a movie so we went with him to get some dinner and talk.

DR. OPAL BANKS. Katie? You are awfully quiet.

KATIE. Amanda tells the story much better than I do.

AMANDA. You can talk if you like, Katie. I don't want to be rude.

KATIE. No, *you* tell it.

AMANDA. He told us that we were special and had so much potential and would go far in Hollywood. And we believed him. That's why we went back to his hotel room… Gosh, if I had only known.

KATIE. I didn't want to go.

DR. OPAL BANKS. And that's when he raped you girls and made the infamous tape that spread like wildfire all over the internet?

KATIE. Yes. He *raped* us. He *raped* us.

AMANDA. I know, Katie. I was there.

KATIE. As long as *you* know.

AMANDA. Dr. Opal, it was so horrible. I wanted to run away and save Katie, but he had a gun. Before he turned the camera on, he pulled out a gun and said he would kill us if we didn't do what he wanted. Oh Dr. Opal, it was the most horrible experience of my life! I felt so guilty that my very best friend in the whole world had to endure that. I wish I could have protected Katie. I wish I could have saved her.

DR. OPAL BANKS. Wow. Katie you are very lucky to have a friend like Amanda.

KATIE. I know I am.

DR. OPAL BANKS. It is so important for me to have all of America hear your story. There are millions of young girls out there who dream of stardom. And there are predators everywhere like Jim Grimes who are capable of preying on the dreams of children. The dreams of OUR children. If you girls could say one thing to all of the young girls and parents watching, what would it be? Just look into the camera and talk to them.

AMANDA. Just focus on school and being a kid because once that is gone you will never get it back. God loves you and has a plan for you and you just have to trust that.

KATIE. You don't have to be famous to be happy. Be happy being an ordinary kid. It isn't so bad.

DR. OPAL BANKS. Well said, girls. Well said. It brings me such joy to know that you two have overcome such a horrific ordeal. You have wonderful parents and a wonderful pastor.

KATIE. He is so wonderful and so loving and so kind. That's why — *(Amanda pipes in, jealous that Katie is stealing the spotlight for a moment.)*

AMANDA. A long time ago, when Katie and I were lost and Pastor Jim showed us the light, we promised him we would do anything to help him—

KATIE. So that's why—

AMANDA. That's why we are wearing these buttons. This is the name of our church, God's Honor Chapel. Pastor Jim asked us to wear these so we could use this horrible ordeal to spread the forgiving word of Jesus. Just like he did when his brother Todd died.

KATIE. You can go online to www.GodsHonorChapel.com and check out Pastor Jim's youth ministries to help avoid temptation and find forgiveness and salvation and purity.

DR. OPAL BANKS. That's wonderful.

KATIE. God works in mysterious ways.

DR. OPAL BANKS. What are you girls plans after you finish high school?

KATIE. I want to be a veterinarian.

AMANDA. I want to be a real actress. I'm going to move to Hollywood and audition for real. Maybe you could help me out, Dr. Opal?

DR. OPAL BANKS. Oh you are adorable. Look me up when you get here. I wish you girls all the luck in the world! You are going to do great things with your lives. Thank you for joining us, ladies. *(Lights out on the girls. Dr. Opal turns to the camera as though she is reading from a cue card.)* Up next we have some shocking footage from a brothel in Bangkok. Some of these girls are as young as five. We also have a child specialist who will teach parents steps they can take to keep their girls safe from sexual exploitation. And if you'd like to discuss any topic on today's show please visit www.DrOpalBanks.com. We'll be right back!

Scene Four

Steps of the church. The girls sit, overwhelmed by the loud voices and commotion of the television crew. After a few moments, the commotion fades and the sounds of trucks driving away fades in the distance. Katie and Amanda both sit in an awkward silence, not really sure what to say to each other.

KATIE. What time is it?

AMANDA. I'm not really sure.

KATIE. Oh… Rob should be here any minute. He just got his driver's license and he promised he would teach me.

AMANDA. That's cool. Are you gonna try out for the school play? It's *Cinderella*. There's a lot of parts.

KATIE. I don't think so. I'm not really interested in that stuff. I don't know. Are you?

AMANDA. Yeah. I've been practicing all week. I've decided I'm gonna move to LA after high school and try this for real, you know? Not the "Frank Miller" way.

KATIE. That's cool.

AMANDA. Do you think she meant what she said about me looking her up when I get to LA?

KATIE. Maybe… I wish you luck.

AMANDA. You should try out for the play. We could do it together. I don't know… I miss you… You are still my best friend. You could spend the night maybe? Like old times? We could watch *The Little Mermaid* and eat potato chips with ketchup and salt. *(Katie smiles for a brief moment.)*

KATIE. Yeah, maybe. I'm just really busy with cheerleading practice and honors classes and Kylie wants me to try out for the dance squad with her and I hardly see Rob since he has football practice…

AMANDA. Sure… sure… *(Awkward silence for a few moments. Katie fidgets with her button.)*

KATIE. I guess you should hear this from me before the rumors start to fly at school…

AMANDA. What?

KATIE. I'm four months pregnant.

AMANDA. What?

KATIE. Yeah… Boy did my and Rob's parents flip… But we all decided the proper Christian thing would be for me and Rob to get married and him to move in with us… I'm really trying to be a good Christian these days…

AMANDA. Wow… You could have called me. *(Sound of a car pulling up.)*

KATIE. That's Rob. I guess I'll see you around at school.

AMANDA. Yeah, I guess. *(Katie gets up to leave, then stops and looks at Amanda.)*

KATIE. Don't worry, Mandy. Someday you'll be famous. Someday you'll be so famous that no one will remember what you got famous for. And me and Rob will take our kids to all your movies and I will tell them that I knew you before you got discovered. I promise. *(Katie spits on her pinky and offers it to Amanda. They latch fingers together. Katie exits. Amanda sits alone on the stage. She folds her hands to pray.)*

AMANDA. Dear God. Please let me be famous. I'll do anything… Amen.

Youth Group Lesson Seven

Flashback. The giggles of children and honking parents outside fades. Pastor Jim surveys the empty room. He smiles to himself. His work here is done.

PASTOR JIM. John 1:5: "And the light shines in darkness; and the darkness has not understood it."

Epilogue
Video Montage One
Hotel Room

The secret tape Amanda made on the infamous night. This should be shown after the curtain call as the audience leaves the theater. The effect is that audience members who see the tape may have a different opinion of the girls than audience members who do not see the tape. The camera is hidden in Amanda's backpack. We see her open the bathroom door and the floor and Frank's feet as she emerges. She strategically places the backpack on a chair so that we can see the bed and Frank's camera. Katie is sitting there smiling. Amanda plops down on the bed.

FRANK. Are you ladies ready to have some fun?

KATIE. Do we do our dance routine for the camera?

AMANDA. Do we read from a script or something? I read online that at auditions you read from scripts.

FRANK. How famous do you ladies want to be?

AMANDA. Very famous.

FRANK. Willing to do whatever it takes?

KATIE. Ummm…

FRANK. Strip for me. *(We see Frank's face for the first time. He is very handsome.)*

KATIE. I… I don't want to.

FRANK. This is what everyone in Hollywood does. Miley Cyrus, Lindsay Lohan, Nicole Richie, Paris Hilton, Britney Spears, the Olsen twins, and on and on and on.

AMANDA. Really? But I read in *Cosmo Girl* that you do screen tests in Hollywood —

FRANK. This is a screen test. This is what everyone does in Hollywood.

KATIE. But… Everyone?

FRANK. Everyone.

AMANDA. Even the ones who talk about Jesus?

FRANK. I pray to Jesus every single day.

KATIE. Really?

FRANK. Of course. My favorite Bible quote is John 3:16. Do you girls know that quote?

KATIE. That's our pastor's favorite quote.

FRANK. "For God so loved the world that he gave his one and only Son, that whoever believes in Him shall not perish but have eternal life."

KATIE. Wow.

FRANK. Now strip for me.

AMANDA. I don't…

FRANK. I thought there was something special in you both, but maybe I am wrong. You'll never make it in Iowa let alone Hollywood if you aren't willing to go above and beyond. *(Frank opens the door to show them out.)* Bus station is down the street.

AMANDA. Please don't. I am willing to do what it takes. *(Amanda looks at Katie.)*

KATIE. It's a sin, Amanda. We should go.

AMANDA. I have to do this.

KATIE. We're not even old enough to be here. We're only fourteen—

AMANDA. Shut up, Katie!

FRANK. I already saw your I.D.s. You can't pull that trick on me. I know you girls are eighteen. If you girls trust me, you will be the brightest stars in Hollywood. But you have to have faith in me. Do you trust me?

AMANDA. Yes.

KATIE. I'm not sure… *(Frank sits down next to Katie. He studies her face.)*

FRANK. You are such a beautiful girl.

KATIE. Really?

FRANK. Your mouth… Your eyes… I'm sure you hear that all the time.

KATIE. Well… Not really.

FRANK. What a shame. You're the most beautiful creature… The world needs to appreciate your beauty. You're far more beautiful than Megan Fox and look at how the world worships her… Do you trust me?

KATIE. OK. *(Both girls undress.)*

FRANK. We're gonna make the greatest movie ever. *(Frank turns on his camera.)*

KATIE. You really think I'm beautiful?

FRANK. I think you are the most beautiful creature that ever walked the face of this planet. Now kiss me down there… *(Katie hesitates for a moment, then she gets down on her knees and unzips Frank's pants. Amanda watches.)*

AMANDA. What about me?

FRANK. I think you are destined to be the biggest star the world has ever seen.

AMANDA. Promise? *(Frank nods.)*

FRANK. Welcome to Hollywood, ladies.

AMANDA. Jesus will forgive us. Jesus will forgive us. Jesus will forgive us. *(Amanda gets down on her knees. LIGHTS OUT.)*

END OF PLAY

Reviews of *American Girls*

"*American Girls* is a thought-provoking, squirm-inducing, very funny meditation on sexual politics among America's youth, and I highly recommend it…. Hilary Bettis has written an important and fascinating play, and she is without doubt a writer and performer to keep an eye on." — nytheatre.com

"…the play's concept is strong, and the two leads perfectly portray young teenagers with adult ambitions. Katie's constant reminders to 'stop using the Lord's name in vain' make us realize just how naïve the girls really are, ultimately tying *American Girls* together as an interesting and thought-provoking work." — showbusinessweekly.com

"…a surprising and original new voice is making its debut. It would have been so easy to make this merely an issue-of-the-week-type play railing against the sexual exploitation of young girls — a pretty easy target. Instead, Bettis gives us something more interesting — a world where the lines between victimhood and single-minded striving for glory are blurred. American girls — and boys — haven't heard the last from this impressive young writer." — newyorkcool.com

"There's a palpable power dynamic between Amanda, the leader, who can justify anything as God's plan, and the sensitive, fearful Katie, who shares the I'll-do-anything dream but knows that something isn't right… Bettis gives an entertaining, perceptive tour of the confused middle-school mindset." — backstage.com

"Bettis' dialogue is note-perfect, capturing the hilariously banal concerns of day-to-day school life, as well as the girls' hunger for fame ... great first play from Bettis." — broadwayworld.com

Author's Note

American Girls is a play full of land mines. It is a play whose power can be easily destroyed with one false move. With that in mind, a little navigation from the playwright...

Amanda and Katie are real girls. They are real, plain, average, ordinary girls. They are not the prettiest girls in the room. Far from it. They are the plain little girls in the corner that most people never notice. Their bodies are average at best. They have baby fat. They have real breasts. They are going through puberty. They do not look like movie stars or ingénues or prom queens or porn stars. They never will. They will grow up to be plain women. Just like the vast majority of us. This is NOT a story about the ugly duckling. I repeat myself; this is NOT a story about the ugly duckling.

Amanda and Katie are real girls. They are good at math. They get good grades. They have hopes and dreams and fears and crushes. Their parents love them and they love their parents. They come from good homes. They are deeply vulnerable, deeply confused, and deeply desperate to feel valued in their world. That is the point of the play. They are not "valley girls" or ditsy or airheads or dumb. They do not talk like that. Please give them depth and honesty and empathy. They deserve that. We must love them. We must see our own children in them.

Pastor Jim is a decent man. He is filled with ghosts and demons. He truly believes that he must save these children by leading them to Christ. He is charming and kind and genuine and soft-spoken. The children love him. The parents love him. We must see why they love him. We must love him. We must want to believe him. We must want to be saved too.

Frank is not sinister. He is gorgeous. He is probably the most attractive man the girls will ever be with. His power is his looks. And when his face is revealed at the end we must understand why the girls were putty in his hands.

Be very careful with the technology used in this play. It must not overshadow the action on stage. It is there to heighten the struggle between this paradise called Hollywood and this paradise called Heaven. The girls are torn.

This play must be treated with subtlety, integrity, and honesty from the actors and director. There is a ton of humor and sadness and irony and exploitation. Do not emphasize it. The audience is intelligent. They will see it. Understatement is the most powerful tool you have.

Property List

Video camera (AMANDA)
Red lipstick (KATIE)
Retainer (AMANDA)
Glasses (AMANDA)
Hello Kitty headband (AMANDA)
Pixie Sticks candy (BOTH GIRLS)
Ad from internet (BOTH GIRLS)
Cell phone (AMANDA)
Picture (BOTH GIRLS)
Pencils (BOTH GIRLS)
Notebooks (BOTH GIRLS)
Makeup (BOTH GIRLS)
Backpacks (BOTH GIRLS)
Matching "Pixie Chicks" outfits (BOTH GIRLS)
Cloth to remove makeup (BOTH GIRLS)
Sunglasses (BOTH GIRLS)
Heels (BOTH GIRLS)
Magazines (BOTH GIRLS)
Lotion (AMANDA)
Stuffed elephant (BOTH GIRLS)
Bible (AMANDA)
"Our Big Break" box (AMANDA)
Video tape (AMANDA)
Scissors (AMANDA)
Tissues (PASTOR JIM AND BOTH GIRLS)
Empty tissue box (BOTH GIRLS)
"God's Honor Chapel" buttons (BOTH GIRLS)
Ear piece (BOTH GIRLS)
Small microphone (BOTH GIRLS)

Masterpiece
by M. Z. Ribalow

Masterpiece was developed at New River Dramatists, a Garden of Eden for playwrights, certainly this one. There were many people contributing to the readings of this play, but special thanks to those who were involved in more than one of its incarnations: Randell Haynes, Richmond Hoxie, Tom Kleh, John W. Love Jr., Michael Medeiros, Patricia Randell, Victor Slezak and Mark Woods.

Details have been changed, but this is a true story.

This play is dedicated to Patricia Randell, whose performances have made so many of my plays better than I ever knew they could be.

Cast *(in order of appearance)*
BREDIUS Fifties or sixties. An elegant, distinguished, knowledgeable man; educated, enormously self-assured, prone to being blinded by the glare of his own brilliance, and to mistaking his depth of vision for clarity.

JO A woman in her forties. Blazingly intelligent, astute, outspoken. Utterly committed to any cause or person she undertakes as her own. An actress. Artistic and personal integrity, as well as deep passion, are at the very core of her being.

HAN VAN MEEGEREN Male in his 40's. Artistic, ambitious, restless, brooding, driven, charismatic, impulsive, emotional, searching. Looking for love, fame, fortune, glory, and pleasure, and not overly concerned how he achieves them.

WOONING A man of indeterminate age. Calm, quiet, enigmatic, impossible to read or to ruffle. Smarter than you think, more observant than you imagine. Misses nothing. A seeker of truth who cares about little else. You wouldn't want to play poker with him. Ever.

Time: Starts in 1936, ends in 1945.

Place: Various locales in Rotterdam, The Netherlands

Set: A series of rooms in Amsterdam between 1936–1947. Reproductions of particular paintings are projected during various scenes.

ACT I
Scene One

(Rotterdam, The Netherlands, 1936. An art gallery. We see projections of Han van Meegeren's paintings. Abraham Bredius is trying to leave. Jo is stopping him by physically standing in his way. He is somewhere between fifty and sixty, elegant, staggeringly self-assured, a man who never doubts himself. He is upper-class and proud of it. She is in her forties, intelligent, outspoken, passionately devoted to whatever it is that she wants. She is pleading; he is losing patience)

BREDIUS. I've *looked* at it.

JO. But you haven't *seen* it.

BREDIUS. I came, I saw, I was depressed.

JO. Please look again.

BREDIUS. I've *tried* to like it. I *want* to like it. I live in hopeful anticipation that some new artist's work will thrill me. That's one reason I get up in the morning.

JO. But van Meegeren's paintings…

BREDIUS. I also want to like them for your sake, Jo. I adore you. I adored you when you were married to my colleague who didn't deserve you, I adored you when you left him, and I adore you now. Don't you know I would praise your new beau's work in any way I honestly could, if only for your benefit?

JO. So…

BREDIUS. But I can't. I just can't. *(He glances at it, then tries to leave again. She still won't let him)*

JO. It's *art*.

BREDIUS. It's *bad* art.

JO. According to you.

BREDIUS. Why should I care about anyone's judgment but my own?

JO. The artist could say the same thing.

BREDIUS. And he should.

JO. But van Meegeren *has* to care what you think. *Your* opinion becomes Holland's opinion.

BREDIUS. That's because Holland *needs* my opinion. If we were to take seriously work like this, what would be the point of praising Caravaggio? Indeed, what would be the point of *being* Caravaggio?

JO. You're being unfair.

BREDIUS. "Unfair"? (*beat*) Jo, my life changed forever when I first saw Michelangelo's work. To know what human beings are capable of creating at their most inspired... Some people worship sex or money or glory. What makes *me* weep with rhapsody is contemplating da Vinci. Having standards gives life its meaning. To praise mediocrity demeans talent and insults genius.

JO. I find van Meegeren's work haunting, soulful and moving.

BREDIUS. That's because you're sleeping with him.

JO. I don't think Han is talented because I sleep with him. On the contrary. I sleep with him because of his talent.

BREDIUS. Don't let anyone else know. There's no point being considered pathetic when everyone is willing to see you as tragic.

JO. His paintings affect me.

BREDIUS. Rembrandt makes me *feel*. Magritte makes me *think*. Picasso makes me *see*. Han van Meegeren just reminds me that there should be a talent test for anyone claiming to be an artist. Nothing is as stultifying to the spirit as adequate art. The very phrase is an oxymoron. (*He walks over to it as if he is going to reach out and grab it, but he doesn't*) If I burned this right now, it would be more useful keeping us warm than it will ever be as a work of art.

JO. Perhaps I see something that you are missing.

BREDIUS. My artistic conscience will not allow me to treat *merde* as *mousse*. Pardon my language.

JO. I pardon your language. I don't pardon your lack of generosity and understanding.

BREDIUS. Jo, you are an actress. A real one, with talent. When some pretty girl walks around a stage pretending her breasts are actresses, do you think we should take her seriously?

JO. I always loved your intelligence.

BREDIUS. And I yours.

JO. But you're too critical. That always makes me keep a certain emotional distance from you.

BREDIUS. Without a certain emotional distance, one cannot see a creation clearly, much less know its true value.

JO. The whole point is to believe in someone's worth and potential without them having to prove it to you first.

BREDIUS. You're talking about faith, Jo. That was always the river that left us on separate shores. That buffoon, Hitler, currently in the process of destroying the world as we know it — for whom you have the same contempt *I* do — is followed by millions of the faithful. If enough of them shared my preference for informed truth over blind faith, the world would be a better place. Not to mention safer.

JO. Han has the right to believe in his own work.

BREDIUS. But does he have the right to make the rest of us look at it? Can't he just hang it on his wall and leave the world in peace?

JO. The authorities rejected Jesus, too.

BREDIUS. Han van Meegeren is not Jesus, darling. He's not even Barabbas.

JO. You could be wrong, you know.

BREDIUS. The hour it took me to look at this derivative drivel is an hour I will never have again. I could have spent it listening to Mozart or reading Shakespeare. If there *is* a god who put us here for any purpose, *dreck* like this cannot possibly be that reason. Life is too short to spend it on anything less worthwhile than seeking the sublime. (*He exits. She remains there a moment, musing, as the lights fade to black and the scene ends*)

ACT I
Scene Two

(*Han's studio. Paintings, tables and easels are scattered about. Han and Jo are in the afterglow of deeply satisfying sex, still caressing each other*)

HAN. You know, I was thinking…

JO. *I* wasn't.

HAN. …that the only critic in Paradise was a snake.

JO. Yes, but if that silly bitch had just ignored his opinion about apples, we'd still be there.

HAN. You're right. You're right because you're wonderful. You're wonderful because you're right. Who cares about the rest of them, anyway?

JO. Let's just be happy, you and I. After all, happiness is the best revenge.

HAN. They have everything except talent. And you. They don't have you. The poor pathetic bastards. What a miserable existence it must be without talent or you.

JO. You make me so happy when you ignore everyone's criticism but mine.

HAN. You know why I'm so giddy with delight?

JO. Your mad passion for me? Your unshakeable belief in your own work?

HAN. Actually, it's this. (*He rises, points to something on the table and hands her a large magnifying glass. She gets up and looks through it at the canvas on the table, which we see projected on a backstage screen. He speaks with impassioned enthusiasm*)

HAN. You see the cracks in the canvas?

Jo. What about them?

Han. Crackle! (*erotically enthralled*) With the oils of the old masters, it could take over fifty years before the evaporation process was complete.

Jo. Why are you telling me things I know?

Han. You like my doing that when we're in bed.

Jo. That's sex.

Han. So is this.

Jo. (*beat*) Then continue, by all means.

Han. During the long drying process, the diminishing amount of paint on the canvas causes cracks to appear.

Jo. And the unintended hairlines authenticate the period in which the work was painted. Yes, I know. My former husband was an art critic, as you may recall.

Han. These subtle signs of aging give the painting a much greater value. Just as you, sweetheart, are so much more mesmerizing now than you were when I first met you.

Jo. Are you trying to convince me that my wrinkles make me more desirable?

Han. Your face reflects the intricacies of the life you've lived. Your beauty was always compelling. Now it is sublime. (*Jo leans over and kisses him gently but with considerable passion. When the kiss finally breaks, he smiles at her*)

Han. So what would you say is the period of this canvas?

Jo. (*looks hard*) Seventeenth century?

Han. Precisely.

Jo. So what's special about it?

Han. It is three days old.

Jo. (*beat*) How is that possible?

Han. The miracle of chemistry. Thirty years ago, an American invented a synthetic liquid that made surfaces extremely hard.

Jo. Americans seem able to invent anything except the wisdom to control their inventions.

Han. The primary elements of the liquid are phenol and formaldehyde. It occurred to me that if I applied a compound of the two to a canvas, it might mimic the aging process of a centuries old painting. It does — without affecting the colors of the pigments!

Jo. What are you talking about?

Han. Jo, you will soon see a truly astonishing sight: a previously unknown painting of Jan Vermeer.

Jo. How in the world... oh. My God. Are you mad?

Han. That *is* an interesting question, isn't it?

Jo. Han. No one believes in your talent more than I. But you are not, nor ever will be, Jan Vermeer.

Han. I'm not trying to be. I'm just going to show the world what fools critics really are. I will forge a Vermeer that will be hailed as a lost masterpiece.

Jo. You can't seriously expect to get away with that.

Han. It wouldn't be the first time, and it won't be the last. Look. When a possible discovery of an Old Master comes up, how do experts decide whether it's real?

Jo. The quality of the painting, of course. And the subject. How it's approached, and handled.

Han. Exactly. That and the age of the canvas.

Jo. You don't think they'll question the age?

Han. The age will be what convinces them! It will seem exactly right. And they'll never look for this compound. They're critics, remember, not creative people. They look for familiar elements, not inventive technique. They'll examine the south thinking it's cold because the wind is whistling up their ass from the north.

Jo. But the picture itself...

Han. Vermeer is perfect for my purpose. Not only is he a master, but he himself was dismissed by the critics of his own time as trivial. His early work might easily have been discarded as unimportant. Unappreciated genius is nothing new.

JO. But if you try to copy his early work…

HAN. Not copy. Emulate. It has to be something Vermeer might have done before he *became* Vermeer.

JO. This is lunacy.

HAN. Yes. I should have thought of it much sooner.

JO. What are you considering as a subject?

HAN. Christ. At a supper.

JO. But Vermeer never painted religious subjects.

HAN. Except once. "The Christ in the House of Martha and Mary."

JO. Which many think was the work of Jan van der Meer of Utrecht, not Jan Vermeer of Delft.

HAN. Only because it doesn't resemble anything Vermeer ever did. It's neither what he painted nor how he painted it. It's absurd that anyone attributes it to Vermeer. Yet most people do. Do you know *why*?

JO. Lord God. Bredius.

HAN. Yes. Lord God Bredius. He found the painting in a London shop, decided he "saw Vermeer in it," and convinced society's sheep that Vermeer had at some point gone to Italy and been influenced by the Italians. But if he had, of course…

JO. There would be other paintings.

HAN. One would think so.

JO. And there aren't.

HAN. No one's ever found one. And no one in this entire world is more anxious to find one than our favorite art expert, Abraham Bredius.

JO. He's an enemy of your aesthetic. He's not a fool.

HAN. He's like all of us; he sees what he chooses to see. And I am absolutely certain that he will choose to see Vermeer in my painting. All I have to do is make it *suggest* Vermeer without making it too much like the real thing. The thought of a major discovery will overpower Bredius.

JO. He'll check every aspect of the canvas.

HAN. I'm painting over an actual seventeenth century canvas. Got it cheap from a Jewish dealer who's selling stock while he still can.

JO. The paints themselves...

HAN. Vermeer's. I'm recreating them. The lapis lazuli is a challenge. I have to grind it by hand myself.

JO. If you've overlooked anything, Han — anything at all, even the most trivial detail...

HAN. I haven't.

JO. ...they will attack you with merciless, total abandon.

HAN. I would prefer even that to what I suffer at their hands now: condescension and indifference.

JO. If you don't fool him...

HAN. My intention is to let him fool himself. That's the incomparably delicious sauce I will pour over his humiliated head while he cooks his own goose.

JO. May I ask how he's going to become aware of this unknown masterpiece?

HAN. Well. If a reputable art aficionado whom he trusts was shown it by a Jewish family forced to sell their estate...

JO. I'll be more ruined than *you* will. It will destroy my reputation for integrity.

HAN. You knew nothing about it.

JO. Who is going to believe that?

HAN. Everyone. Once they realize I've made fools of them, they will certainly accept that I've betrayed a helplessly infatuated actress. They will do anything to not believe that you, as well as I, have made them look like the idiots they are.

Jo. Are you *that* sure you've thought of everything?

Han. I am sure that *they* will not. I count on the vanity and ambition of society's most esteemed critic. I don't see how I can go wrong doing that.

Jo. I beg you to consider the risk.

Han. I beg you to consider the reward.

Jo. Han. This is terrifying.

Han. Yes. Will you do it?

Jo. And throw away every scruple I have?

Han. I cannot do this without you.

Jo. When I said I'd follow you anywhere, I did not mean over the edge into an abyss.

Han. I will protect you at every turn. As Vermeer pours light through his windows into his interiors, that's how you illuminate mine.

Jo. They'll crucify you.

Han. They do that now. They just call it reviewing my work.

Jo. Isn't there —

Han. No.

Jo. Not a —

Han. None.

Jo. Well. Then I'll have to say no. (*pause*) Unless I say yes.

Han. I adore you.

Jo. You'd better, if I'm crazy enough to do this.

Han. I do.

Jo. I believe you.

Han. You do much more than that. You believe *in* me.

Jo. Yes. I do. And to show the whole world how great an idiot a critic can be… that is a difficult temptation for an actress to resist.

HAN. *(gets down on one knee and takes her hand)* Will you marry me?

JO. Yes. *(beat)* If you're not in prison on the wedding day. *(The lights fade to black and the scene ends)*

ACT I
Scene Three

(Spring 1937 — more than half a year later. Han and Jo are in Han's studio. She is staring raptly at his painting, while he alternates his attention between his work and her reaction to it. He's equal parts confident, triumphant and anxious. He's as intense as he's ever felt, and it shows. She is stunned by what she sees. Van Meegeren's painting "The Supper at Emmaus" is projected on a large screen so that the audience is able to see what Jo sees)

JO. It's amazing.

HAN. But is it good?

JO. Yes.

HAN. Does it look like it might have been done by the same Vermeer who didn't paint "The Christ in the House of Martha and Mary" either?

JO. Well…

HAN. The Emmaus story has rarely been done, but Caravaggio painted *two* versions. Bredius will jump at that — it will suggest that Vermeer went to Italy and was influenced by Caravaggio, though there's no evidence of that whatsoever. The "Martha and Mary" is the only supposed Vermeer with almost life-size figures — another reason it wouldn't *be* Vermeer — so I've made these figures proportional to them. I've put in just enough similarities so that they'll be consumed debating the aesthetic, instead of noticing that the painting itself isn't genuine.

JO. And if they look deeper?

HAN. I painted over a canvas from Vermeer's own period. "The Raising of Lazarus." The work of some minor artist. I used the original stretcher. Even seventeenth century *tacks*. If it was any more authentic to the period, Vermeer would be joining us for lunch.

Jo. Christ's hands...

Han. *(suddenly anxious)* What about them?

Jo. They're wonderful. Long, strong, delicate.

Han. Oh. Yes. They are, aren't they? Thank you.

Jo. It's your best work, Han.

Han. It isn't really mine, though, is it?

Jo. Of course it is. It's not a copy of anything, is it?

Han. It doesn't even resemble anything the man painted.

Jo. Which makes it an original. Doesn't it?

Han. Well. Yes. You're right.

Jo. Quite different from your own — your other — work. Especially your sexually provocative ones. Which shocked some. And aroused others.

Han. I remember your response to "I Have Summoned Up the Depths." And my response to your response.

Jo. Feel like re-creating that reaction? *(Their attention is now entirely on each other, the painting momentarily forgotten)*

Han. Germany banned that one for being pornographic.

Jo. Yes.

Han. I didn't think it was.

Jo. Nor I. But it was close enough to be my favorite. *(With an effort, she looks away from him and back at the painting)* Until now.

Han. Thank you.

Jo. I like the characteristic Vermeer light source. The typical window on the left.

Han. Yes. I've kept it understated, you see.

Jo. I see.

Han. Just a light-colored rectangle. Simply drawn.

Jo. I love you.

HAN. There are subtle parallels to the Caravaggio. The full face of Christ, his downcast eyes, left of center; one unseen man facing Jesus, the other gazing at Christ in profile. Of course, I've made sure there are differences too. This is, after all, the Dutchman, not the Italian. *(beat)* I love you, too. I cannot tell you how much.

JO. You can show me.

HAN. And I will. Later.

JO. But not too much later.

HAN. No. *(beat)* So. Do you think...

JO. I don't know. But, yes.

HAN. I believe we're ready for Bredius.

JO. You've always been ready for him. He's just never been ready for you.

HAN. God, Jo. Won't it be wonderful when...

JO. Yes. Now we'll see. *(beat)* We'll see. *(They both stare at the painting. The lights fade to black as the scene ends)*

ACT I
Scene Four

(Summer 1937, a month or so later. Bredius and Jo are in Bredius's residence. He is holding a glass carefully, regarding the liquid in it as if it is indescribably precious. She holds a similar glass, from which she sips)

JO. This brandy is exquisite.

BREDIUS. Do you know, I once met a philistine who threw away a glass of the most wonderful brandy because he preferred beer. *(beat)* I loved my mother.

JO. Of course you did.

BREDIUS. She was the most precious thing in the world to me, as I was to her. When as a child I buried my face in her neck, the scent of her was like... bliss. This brandy tastes the way she smelled. The purest ambrosia. Do you know, I am sure that at the moment of my death, my last vision will be something of unbearable beauty.

JO. I did come to discuss the painting.

BREDIUS. We *are* discussing the painting. Brandy and beer. Although there are some beers that are quite good, for what they are.

JO. In my heart, I always felt you would be able to sense the truth about its authenticity.

BREDIUS. Of course you did. You and I, Jo — we always respond intuitively to what is genuine in art.

JO. And this painting… *(During this scene, he refers to, stares at, and examines the painting, which faces upstage. We still see it projected to us)*

BREDIUS. There is not the slightest question about this painting. The *pointilles* in the bread and elsewhere could only have been done by the great master. It is as good as a signature; as soon as I saw the bread, I no longer had any doubts. This is a triumph of the early Jan Vermeer.

JO. *(beat)* But the religious theme. It wasn't what he painted.

BREDIUS. Of course it was. We just hadn't yet *found* it. Now I have.

JO. I just wouldn't want you to be mistaken about something so important.

BREDIUS. Mistaken? I am touched by your concern, Jo — truly I am — but I? Mistaken? About a Vermeer? Please!

JO. But couldn't it be someone else's work?

BREDIUS. No.

JO. Or even… a fake of some kind?

BREDIUS. Don't be ridiculous. If someone wanted us to think this was a Vermeer, he would have made it look like Vermeer's other work. Why fake something so atypical of the master? Besides, look at the ultramarine of Christ's garment. That was Vermeer's special color — his lapis lazuli. Who could reproduce his use of it? And look at the crackle! Authentic, beyond a doubt! Jo, this is the culmination of my life's work. This painting is the holy grail we all seek. The stuff that dreams are made of.

JO. Perhaps it is.

BREDIUS. How can I ever repay you?

JO. You already have. With your authentication.

BREDIUS. I will make sure your role in its discovery is mentioned.

JO. No, my friends must remain anonymous. If the Fascists knew that this had been smuggled out of Italy… you know how they and the Nazis prize great art. My friends' lives would be worth no more than if they were Jews. And I value their lives as pricelessly as I do this painting.

BREDIUS. You are a remarkable woman.

JO. I do concede that possibility. But the credit must be yours. I myself would never have assumed this was the genuine article.

BREDIUS. So you do not mind if *I* announce this myself? It would mean so much to me.

JO. It's *your* discovery. That's the way it *should* be. *(The lights go out on his place, and up on a spotlight, into which Bredius moves, addressing the audience, as a convention of art historians, scholars, critics and other experts)*

BREDIUS. This glorious work of Vermeer, the great Vermeer of Delft, has emerged — thank God! — from the darkness where it lay for many years, undefiled, and just as it left the artist's studio. Its subject is almost unique in its *oeuvre*; a depth of feeling springs from it such as is found in no other work of his. I found it hard to contain my emotions when this masterpiece was first shown to me and many will feel the same who have the privilege of beholding it. Composition, expression, color — all combine to form a unity of the highest art and beauty. Gentlemen of the art world, of the entire world: behold the Master's masterpiece! *(The lights fade, until there is a light only upon the painting itself. Then, a blackout. End of scene)*

Act I
Scene Five

(Spring 1938. Almost a year later. Han and Jo are in their living room. He is sitting, a book in his hand at which he occasionally glances. She is on her feet, clearly emotional)

Jo. I don't know what will happen to me.

Han. But you're my wife.

Jo. When a wife walks out of her husband's house, as I'm walking out of yours right now, he's completely free. You're not bound to me any more. Nor I to you. We're both completely free. Look, here's your ring. Give me mine.

Han. That as well?

Jo. That as well.

Han. Here it is.

Jo. It's finished, then. I'll leave my keys.

Han. Will you ever think of me?

Jo. I'll think of you often.

Han. Can I write to you?

Jo. No. I won't allow that.

Han. Can I at least send you —

Jo. Nothing. Nothing.

Han. Let me help you if you need help —

Jo. No! I'm telling you, I take nothing from strangers.

Han. Am I nothing but a stranger to you, Nora? *(She stops, shifts her stance and tone)*

Jo. You changed some of the lines.

Han. Not really.

Jo. Yes. Really.

Han. Perhaps a slight paraphrase here and there.

Jo. No paraphrase is ever slight. You know that.

Han. I was just giving you your cues. What did I say that would make any —

Jo. My ring.

Han. You mean Nora's ring.

Jo. Hers and mine. Ours. You said "That as well?"

Han. So?

Jo. The correct line is "That too?"

Han. Does it make that much of a difference?

Jo. It forced me to say "as well" as well. Instead of "too," which is the word in the script you're holding, is it not?

Han. Don't they mean the same...

Jo. "Too" has two meanings to it.

Han. Ah.

Jo. There is the possibility that Ibsen knew what he was doing.

Han. It is a translation, after all. Not his exact words.

Jo. They are the exact words that inform the role I inhabit on stage. Each word is sacred text.

Han. Sorry. I'll pay more attention.

Jo. Just pay more respect to the work.

Han. You're taking this all a bit... personally, don't you think?

Jo. If I don't take it personally, who am I? You and I are artists, Han. We don't take anything impersonally.

Han. Except perhaps the odd forgery.

Jo. *(beat)* You're planning another one?

Han. I'm still painting what I feel. The only difference is that I'm pretending to be someone else.

Jo. It's a bit odd to be the wife of the man you love who isn't sure whether he's the man you married.

Han. I'm the same man. Just a different painter. In a way.

Jo. But you faked that painting to make a point.

Han. And I made it, didn't I? But do we really need to sacrifice all this free good fortune? And with the Nazis on the march, shouldn't we get the most out of every moment we have?

Jo. You're going to continue to tempt fate?

Han. I'm not tempting fate, Jo. I'm embracing it. I hope that wherever Vermeer is, he enjoys contemplating the huge sums he receives for my work on his posthumous behalf.

Jo. You're really going to do another Vermeer?

Han. Think how happy we'll make Bredius. More newly discovered Vermeers with religious subjects. We're helping people have faith in God. Is that really such a bad thing?

Jo. And you, Han? What do *you* have faith in?

Han. I have faith in art, love and you. In a god who allows me to create, lets me live with you and invents mountains, rivers, Rembrandt and sex. In your wit and my talents and the Lenkiewicz Bakery's Chocolate Decadence Cake and Bach's violin sonatas and the way your lips meet mine when you're happy and the songs your eyes sing when you're excited and anything that makes our lives together a romantic adventure.

Jo. And you think more forgeries will enrich our lives?

Han. Won't they?

Jo. Only on the surface.

Han. There's a lot to be said for surfaces. We do live on them.

Jo. But we don't live *for* them.

Han. Don't worry, Jo. I know that life doesn't owe us anything, but that's no reason it shouldn't treat us both with the affection and respect we deserve. Anyway — if God didn't mean humans to be such fools, then he wouldn't have made us all so foolish, now would he? *(Lights fade to black as scene ends)*

ACT I
Scene Six

(Two weeks later. Bredius is admiring "The Supper at Emmaus," which is projected to the audience on a screen. Han enters the gallery, stands near him, and acts as though he is evaluating the painting as well)

HAN. Professor Bredius.

BREDIUS. Do I know you, sir?

HAN. Han van Meegeren. The artist.

BREDIUS. Of course. The man who paints on canvases. You're married to Jo now, yes? You are certainly a fortunate man in some areas.

HAN. I can't deny it.

BREDIUS. What brings you here today, van Meegeren?

HAN. To be honest, I heard you were going to be here.

BREDIUS. I had no idea you were desirous of my company.

HAN. I'm not. But I wanted to hear your thoughts concerning the "Emmaus."

BREDIUS. Really? I didn't know you valued my opinion.

HAN. It is of the greatest interest to me.

BREDIUS. Well then. What do I think of a masterpiece by one of our greatest masters? I think it's masterful. Does that surprise you?

HAN. It just doesn't appear to me that Vermeer painted it.

BREDIUS. Of course he painted it. Have you seen my article on the painting's discovery and the reasons for my authentication?

HAN. I couldn't stop reading it.

BREDIUS. And you still have doubts?

HAN. Well. Yes.

BREDIUS. Why?

HAN. Well. Even if the canvas *is* seventeenth century…

BREDIUS. Which it is.

HAN. It doesn't look like his work.

BREDIUS. That's what proves it's his. I explained that.

HAN. Some other painter of that period could just as easily have done it.

BREDIUS. And signed Vermeer's name exactly as he later did?

HAN. Couldn't the signature be fake?

BREDIUS. Even if some imposter had possessed that level of skill, why on earth would anyone have pretended to be an unimportant painter?

HAN. Unimportant? Vermeer?

BREDIUS. Come now, you surely know that his genius was only realized long after he died. By an art historian and critic, of course. His contemporaries refused to realize his greatness. Blithering idiots, wouldn't you agree?

HAN. I certainly would.

BREDIUS. Look, van Meegeren, as a competent craftsman yourself…

HAN. You surprise me. You've never said a favorable word about my work.

BREDIUS. I've never denied that you have a basic talent that enables you to draw with the requisite skill. I just never liked what you chose to paint or how you chose to paint it.

HAN. I appreciate your honesty.

BREDIUS. A man who is dishonest about his art is the lowest form of life. He's worse than a man who cheats at solitaire. But consider: if I asked you to copy this painting, and gave you the appropriate colors and canvas, do you think you could reproduce it?

HAN. Yes.

BREDIUS. Precisely? With a similarity so unerring that it might at a cursory glance be taken as the original?

HAN. Yes.

BREDIUS. So do I.

HAN. *(genuinely surprised)* Really?

BREDIUS. Absolutely. You have fundamental skills, even a modicum of talent. But would your copy, however slavishly perfect, have the effect of this original? Never. Because you could never hope to capture the personal vision, the spiritual power of the real thing. You would be imitating, not truly expressing, the exquisitely vulnerable soul of a real artist. You might be a good fake, even a great one, but a fake you would be. And even if you sold it to a collector who paid you well, even if you took satisfaction from the craft the copy demanded, you would be no more than an applauded mimic, not an artist with anything of your own worth saying.

HAN. *(He didn't expect this)* I see why Jo respects you.

BREDIUS. Everyone respects me. I am not who I am because people like me, you know. They don't, nor should they. But they *do* know that when I give them an opinion, it is my own informed belief, not anyone else's preference. I may on occasion be wrong — though those occasions are rare — but I am a man of adamantine conviction. You may count on that.

HAN. I will. *(beat)* Well, perhaps you are right that this should be considered a genuine Vermeer by the whole world. After all, who am I to argue with the experts?

BREDIUS. You're not a bad fellow, van Meegeren. I admire your willingness to acknowledge true greatness in art. It can't be easy for someone with no more talent than you have to appreciate a true master. I salute you for that generosity of spirit.

HAN. And I congratulate you on your discovery of this extraordinary painting.

BREDIUS. Thank you. But in all honesty, it humbles me. After all, I can only appreciate it. I would give anything — my fame, my money, my life itself — if I could just once paint something this good. I know it's a dream — a fantasy — but as an unremarkable artist yourself, you must feel the same way sometimes. Don't you? *(Han doesn't answer. They both look at the painting. Lights fade to black as the scene ends)*

ACT I
Scene Seven

(June 1943, five years later. Han is tossing darts at a dartboard with Hitler's face as the target. The surroundings are now visibly richer; they are living in a lavish mansion. Still, his activity should suggest a bored restlessness. Jo enters, returned from a trip to the outside world. She is agitated)

JO. You sold it yourself?

HAN. What difference does it make? The dealer assured me that it's going straight into a private collection, like most of the others.

JO. After all these years of protecting your identity? There's always a danger that...

HAN. There's never a danger! They don't know, they don't care, they don't even look! God! Five rediscovered Vermeers in less than four years, and they don't even *wonder*? They paid six million guilders without even checking the work! Christ! I always knew they knew nothing, but I had no idea they knew this much *less* than nothing!

JO. When we were less successful, I was never this depressed.

HAN. The details I forged in "The Supper at Emmaus" were brilliant! Every 17th century recreated pigment — and they didn't examine it carefully enough to even notice!

JO. Well, you're certainly not taking that kind of care any more, are you?

HAN. What's the point? "The Last Supper" — the first one, the one I did after "Emmaus" — has a hunting scene with dogs and horsemen underneath the painting I presented as Vermeer's. If they had looked at it under radiography, they would have clearly seen a spaniel sniffing a partridge directly under the figure of Christ! But none of it matters to them!

JO. Not to them, perhaps. It does to me.

HAN. They should care more! Someone should have standards, besides the artist making a mockery of them. It's hardly even a challenge any more. How can you mock something that doesn't even exist?

JO. I'm not worried about what's become of them. I'm worried about what's become of us.

HAN. We're the same as we always were. Nothing has changed except my perspective on the entire world.

JO. Han. I didn't have to leave my husband for you. When I went away with you, we both knew why I was doing it. Do you still know why we're together?

HAN. You're the one who said I would have no difficulty selling "The Adulteress."

JO. And you didn't. But I wouldn't hang it on my own wall. The composition, technique, execution — none of them have been given the attention you gave them in "Emmaus."

HAN. It's not *that* bad. Is it?

JO. You barely removed the underpainting. You hardly bothered with the crackle. And in "The Adulteress," you used cobalt, for God's sake! In a seventeenth century painting! It doesn't even look like a Vermeer forgery any more. It's closer to your own older paintings. And you've given up doing your own work.

HAN. No, I haven't. I'm just doing it under different guises.

JO. You're just forging dead artists! Two paintings in the style of de Hooch as well as the annual rediscovered Vermeer?

HAN. They overpay for them all. If I did my work as myself, no one would buy it.

JO. They'll never appreciate van Meegeren unless you give them van Meegeren to appreciate.

HAN. I'm giving them van Meegeren. They just don't know it.

JO. Don't you see? You're not forging Vermeer any more. You're forging yourself.

HAN. None of it matters! They buy all the fakes. They worship all the forgeries. They don't care what's real or good.

JO. But I do. And you should.

HAN. I wanted recognition, Jo. Applause. Acknowledgment of my genius. Or at least my talent.

Jo. And now you have it...

Han. It's meaningless! If pebbles are given the same value as diamonds, why stalk the earth hunting diamonds?

Jo. Because diamonds are precious, rare and beautiful, and pebbles aren't.

Han. Except to fools and madmen. And they are the ones who rule this world.

Jo. That doesn't mean you have to give in to their madness. You never did before. That's what I loved about us. That's why I trusted you.

Han. I thought you'd be on my side.

Jo. I *am* on your side. *You're* not.

Han. I need you to accept me as I am.

Jo. Tell that to the mirror. Your work has become some mutant strain that is neither Vermeer nor van Meegeren. It's Vermeergeren, and he's not the artist I loved with such passion. He's not the man I married.

Han. I'm the same man. Every day.

Jo. You're not even the same man every night!

Han. What does *that* mean?

Jo. You know what it means. The canvas isn't the only place you're forging your feelings. I'm an actress, remember? Don't you think I know the difference between acted passion and the real thing?

Han. You don't think I want you?

Jo. It's not really me you want any more; it's some conjured memory of me. We once fulfilled each other's fantasies. Now we each fantasize about fulfillment. *(beat)* If I'd wanted to live a lie, Han, I wouldn't have married an artist. *(beat)* It seems to me that we've reached the end of our run.

Han. *(stunned pause)* You're leaving me?

Jo. You've already left both of us.

Han. Now that we're finally rich?

Jo. We're not rich. We just have a lot of money.

HAN. Isn't it better to be wealthy and happy than to be poor and sad?

JO. Are we happy? Were we sad?

HAN. I tried to give you everything. It must have been hell for Vermeer, unable to sell his own work, having to make a living as an art dealer by selling paintings he knew were so vastly inferior to his own, which no one would buy.

JO. I never asked you to be Vermeer. I only asked you to be yourself.

HAN. I wanted to be a success for you.

JO. I married you. That's as successful as anyone could possibly be for me.

HAN. Vermeer died a pauper.

JO. He died Vermeer.

HAN. I gave you chiaroscuro.

JO. But I need the light to be on both of us. *(beat)* I'm getting a divorce. I love you, Han, but I can't live with you any more.

HAN. *(suddenly terrified)* You won't...

JO. Don't worry. I would never betray you. I'll still lie for you. I'll do anything for you except live with you.

HAN. Jo. It's you I need.

JO. If it was me you needed, it would be me you'd have chosen. Instead of... all this.

HAN. But I didn't want it alone.

JO. I'm not abandoning you to the wolves, Han. I'm just letting you feed them by yourself. *(She starts to leave. Han calls after her with frantic urgency. His sky is falling)*

HAN. Jo. *(She stops, goes over to him, ruffles his hair, kisses her finger and puts it on his lips, then turns and goes. He looks after her, bereft)*

ACT I
Scene Eight

(It is now 1945. The living room seems somehow even more lavish, if possible. Neither Han nor Jo is onstage, but a strange man is. Jo enters and stops in surprise when she sees Wooning sitting there calmly)

JO. Oh! I didn't... I... who are you, if you don't mind my asking? And even if you do mind my asking.

WOONING. I'm sorry to have startled you. My name is Wooning. The maid let me in.

JO. She must still be giddy from the celebration. Well, Mr. Wooning, how can I help you?

WOONING. I have an appointment with your husband.

JO. Former husband.

WOONING. Former. And yet here you are.

JO. We're going out to dinner tonight to toast the Allies' victory. Is that all right with you?

WOONING. The recent catastrophe that annihilated the rest of Europe does seem to have left you both peculiarly unscathed.

JO. We have been most fortunate. Believe me, I am keenly aware of it.

WOONING. So is much of Holland.

JO. May I ask your business with my former husband?

WOONING. I'd like to speak with him about a painting.

JO. Of course. Which one?

WOONING. Perhaps I should discuss that with him.

JO. Are you an art expert?

WOONING. Not at all. I gather that *you* are, though.

JO. My first husband was an art critic. That doesn't make me an expert on anything, except possibly my first husband.

WOONING. But you're an artist yourself. I've admired your acting onstage. You were remarkable in that Ibsen last season.

JO. Thank you. But as an artist myself, I don't really critique anyone else's art. I just appreciate skill and admire talent.

WOONING. Your first husband, the art critic, must have taught you a great deal about how to evaluate art.

JO. My first husband taught me many things. Some of them were even what he intended me to learn.

WOONING. You seem to be an interesting woman.

JO. *Seem* to be? You have doubts about it?

WOONING. I have doubts about everything. Always.

JO. May I ask what line of work you're in, Mr. Wooning?

WOONING. You may certainly ask. *(pause)* I'm in inquiries.

JO. Inquiries? About paintings?

WOONING. At present.

JO. But sometimes about other things.

WOONING. Sometimes.

JO. Are you endeavoring to be mysterious?

WOONING. I am endeavoring to be noncommittal.

JO. And why are you doing that? Do you lack passion in your life, Mr. Wooning?

WOONING. I regard myself as quite passionate, actually.

JO. About what? Paintings?

WOONING. No. About being noncommittal. *(Han enters, sees them both there, looks at Wooning without recognition)*

HAN. Jo. You're here already. Did you bring a new friend?

JO. We've only just met. Mr. Wooning apparently has an appointment with you.

HAN. Do we have an appointment, sir?

WOONING. Yes.

HAN. I'm afraid I must have forgotten.

WOONING. You were unaware of it.

HAN. Oh. *(beat)* In that case, perhaps you would explain why you are here.

WOONING. Of course. Han van Meegeren, it is my regrettable duty to inform you that you are under arrest. *(There is a moment of silence, while all three are still. Then Han sighs)*

HAN. Ah.

JO. You're with the police?

WOONING. Yes. Inspector Wooning at your service. I regret the misunderstanding regarding my identity.

JO. That was disgracefully devious of you.

WOONING. I thought it best to wait to identify myself until your former husband had appeared.

JO. Did you.

WOONING. Yes. Had you been aware of my purpose here, you might have attempted to evict me from the premises.

JO. I most certainly would have.

WOONING. And would therefore have caused trouble for yourself that I deemed unnecessary.

HAN. Thank you, Inspector.

JO. Why are you thanking him? Throw him out!

HAN. We can't. Can we, Inspector?

WOONING. I'm afraid not.

HAN. He's just being a gentleman protecting you. I certainly thank him for that. *(to Wooning)* Is this about a painting?

WOONING. Yes.

HAN. May I ask which one?

WOONING. "Christ with the Woman Taken in Adultery."

HAN. "The Adulteress." Of course.

JO. Han, don't say anything.

HAN. What difference does it make now? He would not be here unless they had lots of evidence, would you, Inspector?

WOONING. I might. Your former wife is giving you excellent counsel. But as it happens, you are correct. Our evidence is conclusive, and I doubt that anything you say would make much difference.

HAN. In a way, I'm almost relieved.

WOONING. I can understand that.

HAN. Can you really?

WOONING. Yes. Had I done what you have, I don't know how successfully I could have lived with it.

HAN. Living with it is easy enough, as you can see if you look at our surroundings.

WOONING. They seem opulent. And yet, what you did to obtain them is about to result in your arrest and incarceration. If you don't mind my asking, sir, was it really worth prison? Or worse?

HAN. I don't know. Probably not. Though all of life is a prison in one way or another, don't you think, Inspector?

WOONING. No, I don't. Actual prison is not a metaphor to those in it. It's a brutal reality without a drop of abstract romance. I don't believe you will find it readily interchangeable with your current existence, sir. It's considerably less opulent.

JO. Inspector. You said "prison or worse." What did you mean by "or worse"?

WOONING. Well, I don't want to depress you further, but there is of course the possibility of execution.

HAN. Death?

WOONING. That is the usual result of execution, yes.

JO. Oh my god.

HAN. That's ridiculous.

WOONING. Arguably, but it is nonetheless an accepted form of punishment for crimes considered heinous or extreme.

HAN. But my crime surely isn't that heinous or extreme.

WOONING. Most of the population would likely take issue with you on that point, sir.

HAN. They don't execute people for forging a painting!

WOONING. No, sir, they do not. But you are not being charged with forging a painting.

JO. He's not?

WOONING. No.

HAN. I don't understand. Why are you arresting me, if not for that?

WOONING. You are accused of treason.

JO. Treason?

WOONING. High treason. A crime punishable by death. Most citizens of the Netherlands regard collaboration of any sort with the Nazis as unforgivable; and now that the war has finally come to an end, the anger against those who have profited by such collaboration is palpable. You have many countrymen who have endured terrible suffering, poverty, displacement and death in this war. I assure you that your current opulence is not to your advantage in these circumstances.

HAN. Are you joking?

WOONING. Is there anything about my tone or bearing that suggests in any way whatsoever that I am joking?

JO. All Han does is paint and spend money. How could that be treasonous?

WOONING. You sold a painting. Do you deny that?

HAN. When did selling a painting become a capital crime?

WOONING. When the sale of an irreplaceable national treasure is made to the Nazi leadership.

HAN. The Nazi leadership?

WOONING. This great Dutch painting was recently discovered in a cache of artistic masterworks hidden by the Nazi high command and now in the control of the liberating Allied forces. It had been purchased from a Swiss art dealer — who obtained it from you, sir — by Hermann Goering: Commander in Chief of the Luftwaffe, President of the Reichstag, Hitler's designated successor, and a noted appropriator of priceless art pilfered from other countries. He paid a great deal for it.

JO. What a fool. It wasn't even a good one.

HAN. You're arresting me because you think I sold a Vermeer to the Nazis?

WOONING. There seems little question that that's exactly what you did.

HAN. That's insane.

WOONING. Whether it is or not, you are under arrest for doing it. You'll have to come with me to the station now.

HAN. Inspector, there are any number of regrettable acts in my life of which I might be fairly accused. This is not one of them.

WOONING. You will be given the opportunity to prove that, if you can. *(turns to Jo)* Goodbye, Mrs. van Meegeren. I'm sorry to have deceived you. But it's what I do. *(He takes Han in charge and exits with him. Jo is left standing there, alone, forlorn and stunned. Lights fade to black. End Act I)*

ACT II
Scene One

(1945. The Police station. A different day. A standing, or moving, Wooning is interrogating a seated Han)

HAN. Do you really think I'm a traitor?

WOONING. Not for me to judge. I do really think that you sold an irreplaceable national work of art to the Nazis.

HAN. For my thirty pieces of silver, you mean.

WOONING. Oh, it was considerably more rewarding than that.

HAN. Anyway, I only sold it to the dealer, not to the Germans. Why are you prosecuting *me*?

WOONING. The dealer is Swiss. We can't prosecute him; he doesn't live here. You, on the other hand, do. And you're the one who smuggled it out of our country.

HAN. I didn't sell any national treasure, Wooning.

WOONING. The only problem with that assertion, sir, is that you've already admitted selling it.

HAN. Oh, I sold the painting, certainly. But it was hardly a national treasure.

WOONING. Most people consider original paintings by Vermeer among the greatest of art treasures.

HAN. And I am among them. But "The Adulteress" is not the work of Jan Vermeer.

WOONING. You think not?

HAN. I know not.

WOONING. And your evidence of this is?

HAN. My evidence of this is that I painted it.

WOONING. You.

HAN. Yes. It is my work, and my work alone.

WOONING. *(beat)* You will forgive me if I find that somewhat difficult to believe.

HAN. Of course you do. In your case, it's at least honest ignorance. You don't pretend to be an authority on the subject.

WOONING. The authorities —

HAN. Accept it as a Vermeer. Yes, I know. And you believe them?

WOONING. I don't believe anything except evidence.

HAN. What if I could prove to you that I did forge "The Adulteress"?

WOONING. Can you?

HAN. Yes.

WOONING. How?

HAN. I can tell you what's underneath the canvas if you look.

WOONING. You sold it, sir. You could easily know that from your own examination.

HAN. There are details in the painting that make it inauthentic to anyone who really looks.

WOONING. Any of which might have been added during your restoration.

HAN. Why would I do that?

WOONING. So that if arrested for treason you could make precisely the argument you are making now.

HAN. This is going to be more difficult than I thought.

WOONING. A sentiment that has been expressed by many a criminal before you, sir.

HAN. Inspector Wooning. For almost a decade, I have been painting fake Vermeers all of which have been authenticated as real. I'll identify all of them for you and tell you what to look for in each one. Would that convince you?

WOONING. Not by itself, no.

HAN. Then tell me what would. How can I prove that I am not a traitor, but merely a fraud?

WOONING. Well...

HAN. What? Name it.

WOONING. I know nothing about art.

HAN. Then you are the one man I would most like to convince.

WOONING. But if I brought you a painting...

HAN. How do you mean?

WOONING. A Vermeer. A real one.

HAN. Just don't bring me one of mine.

WOONING. Could you copy it?

HAN. Copy it?

WOONING. Yes. Using your paints, make a flawless copy. Show me an example of what you claim you are able to perform. Would you do that to prove your innocence?

HAN. No.

WOONING. Then with respect, sir, I don't see how…

HAN. It would be too easy.

WOONING. How do you mean?

HAN. Any competent hack could make a copy from the original if he had it in front of him. I'm afraid that doing that would prove nothing.

WOONING. Then you may be out of luck.

HAN. Perhaps not. I'll make you a counterproposal.

WOONING. Go on.

HAN. Take me to my studio and allow me full access to my canvases and paints. Give me enough time, and I will create — just for you — a new Vermeer.

WOONING. You'll what?

HAN. I'll show you how I do it by doing it right in front of you. *(There is a pause as Wooning stares at van Meegeren, who returns his look unflinchingly. Wooning considers before replying)*

WOONING. You'd have to be under guard at all times.

HAN. Bring the whole army. I don't care. I'll paint a new Vermeer for the only man in Holland without a predisposition on the subject. I ask you to judge me.

WOONING. How long will it take?

HAN. Long enough for you to see the truth. How important is that to you?

WOONING. *(beat)* I will have my men take you. I will continue my investigation here. I will give you one month to complete your painting.

HAN. I'll need at least six months.

WOONING. I'll give you two.

HAN. Make it four.

WOONING. Two. Or none at all.

HAN. Two it is. But I'll have to skimp. You won't get multiple layers over the original surface. And I won't age and bake it.

WOONING. I will have my men take you there. I will come regularly and you will explain to me exactly what you are painting, and why that would convince experts that it was genuine.

HAN. Thank you.

WOONING. I warn you, van Meegeren. If I find that you are playing with me, I will make certain that you live only long enough to regret it. *(Han suddenly starts laughing. Wooning is nonplussed)*

WOONING. You find this situation humorous?

HAN. No. Not at all. I'm sorry. Really I am. It's just that I was thinking…

WOONING. What?

HAN. Well… for all these years I secretly yearned for people to appreciate all the artistry I put into my forgeries. So now to be denied credit for my own work, to have people insist that my fake masterpieces are actually genuine… don't you find that at least moderately amusing?

WOONING. I don't find any of this amusing. But I will get to the bottom of it, I assure you.

HAN. It has no bottom. But never mind. Take me home, Wooning, and I will paint you a masterpiece. *(The lights fade to black as the scene ends)*

ACT II
Scene Two

(The Police station. A different day. A pacing Wooning is interrogating a seated Bredius)

WOONING. Thank you for helping with my inquiries. I realize that your time is valuable.

BREDIUS. Your time is valuable as well, sir.

WOONING. It's generous of you to evaluate it in that light. Regarding the painting known as "The Adulteress," attributed to Vermeer — are you aware that van Meegeren claims to have forged it?

BREDIUS. He's liable to say anything to avoid being convicted of treason, isn't he?

WOONING. He offers proof that the work is his.

BREDIUS. Do you seriously think that a nonentity like him could possibly paint something so skillful and profound that the entire art world would believe it to be an original Vermeer?

WOONING. I don't know. You're the expert. You tell me.

BREDIUS. Gladly. The answer is no.

WOONING. So you hold the same opinion as Goering.

BREDIUS. That's a vicious comment, Inspector. I had no idea you could be so malicious.

WOONING. There *are* some things you may not know.

BREDIUS. Inspector. I know a great deal about dressing appropriately and how to dine well, and more than a little about the finer things that make life worth living. I confess to an almost total ignorance about politics, business, and all the other irrelevancies to a cultured and meaningful existence. But I do know everything there is to know about art. Everything.

WOONING. Yet you have been mistaken on occasion, have you not?

BREDIUS. I didn't say I've never been wrong. I said I know everything.

WOONING. Are you familiar with the painter Theo van Wijngaarden?

BREDIUS. Of course. I can't imagine why *you* are, though.

WOONING. In 1928—17 years ago—he found a painting he believed was by Franz Hals. It was certified as authentic by your eminent colleague, Dr. Hofstede de Groot. de Groot was so convinced it was an authentic Hals that he himself arranged for its sale at quite a high price.

BREDIUS. How in God's name do you know all this?

WOONING. You examine paintings to decide their worth. I examine facts to decipher their meaning.

BREDIUS. You think de Groot's error is meaningful?

WOONING. You're certain it was an error?

BREDIUS. I said it was, didn't I?

WOONING. You did indeed. You denounced it as a forgery despite your colleague's certificate.

BREDIUS. The paint was too soft. I told him.

WOONING. And he told you to expect that, because van Wijngaarden and his colleague had warned of softness due to the solvents used in the restoration process. de Groot accepted this.

BREDIUS. He was a fool to do so.

WOONING. Your dismissal of his authentication destroyed any market for the painting. The purchase money had to be returned, and van Wijngaarden was left with a worthless canvas, no money, and a tainted reputation.

BREDIUS. Is there some reason you are resurrecting this *artiste manque*'s unfortunate mistake?

WOONING. Yes. Because after this devastating blow you delivered to Theo van Wijngaarden's life, he visited you at your home. *(Bredius pales and is visibly shaken)* I see you now recall the incident.

BREDIUS. I have endeavored to forget that day.

WOONING. Then I will help you remember. He showed you a painting. After a superficial glance, you called it unquestionably a Rembrandt.

BREDIUS. I wouldn't say it was a superficial glance.

WOONING. Wouldn't you? He did it as a joke to show you up. He employed synthetic pigments and allowed the paint to dry naturally. He described to you an elaborate provenance for the painting, which was entirely false. You checked absolutely none of this. You simply pronounced it a genuine Rembrandt.

BREDIUS. I thought you didn't know anything about paintings.

WOONING. I don't. Then, after you'd authenticated this fake, Theo walked up to it with his palette knife and ripped it to shreds in front of you.

BREDIUS. Are you trying to humiliate me, Inspector? Because you certainly have. Yes, I make mistakes. Not often, but on this occasion, he made me look like a total fool. I can't imagine why you are...

WOONING. Do you recall van Wijngaarden's partner on the restoration of the Hals as well as on the fake Rembrandt?

BREDIUS. Why would I...*(beat)* I see. No. I did not know that van Wijngaarden even *had* a partner in his *déclassé* enterprise. So it was van Meegeren?

WOONING. Yes. Theo was his best friend.

BREDIUS. And this proves... what?

WOONING. It proves nothing. But it demonstrates three facts that support van Meegeren's assertions. First, you are capable of colossal errors of judgment. Second, van Meegeren had previously displayed a streak of mischief and a talent for forgery. And finally, he had a strong personal motive — in addition to your dismissive reviews of his own work — to create a fake tailored to fool you specifically.

BREDIUS. You're not referring to the "Emmaus"?

WOONING. I am.

BREDIUS. Listen to me. I know I've been wrong once or twice in my long and distinguished career. And perhaps he did forge some of the others. All of them, even. But not the "Emmaus." He couldn't possibly have forged that.

WOONING. Why not?

BREDIUS. Because it's a Vermeer. A real one.

WOONING. He says it isn't.

BREDIUS. He's trying to save his neck! Don't you understand that?

WOONING. He's only accused of selling "The Adulteress." If he convinces us he forged it, the treason charge will be dismissed. So explain to me why he would make things worse for himself by claiming to have faked "The Emmaus" as well as "The Adulteress," if he didn't? *(Bredius starts to speak, then stops. He has no answer. Wooning regards him impassively, waiting for a response. Bredius is struck by a sudden thought; though reluctant to discuss it, he cannot keep himself from doing so)*

BREDIUS. You know, when our national museum bought "The Washing of Christ's Feet"—

WOONING. One of van Meegeren's fake Vermeers.

BREDIUS. Possibly... We had seven experts consider and evaluate it. Seven of the most knowledgeable art historians in the world.

WOONING. None of you questioned that it was genuine?

BREDIUS. No one really doubted its authenticity. However...

WOONING. What?

BREDIUS. Well... *(pause)* No one liked it.

WOONING. What do you mean?

BREDIUS. Not a one of us actually liked the picture itself. Van Gelder, Hannema, myself; we all agreed that it was rather an ugly painting.

WOONING. Then why in heaven's name did you recommend that The Rijksmuseum pay one million three hundred thousand guilders for a painting that all its experts disliked?

BREDIUS. Well, we thought...

WOONING. You thought what?

BREDIUS. We were afraid that if we didn't buy it, the Germans would. *(Wooning starts to speak, but this time he is the one who finds no words that are fitting. Bredius just sits there, as the lights fade and the scene ends)*

ACT II
Scene Three

(Six weeks later. Han and Wooning are in Han's studio. Han is working on a large canvas that faces upstage so that he can see it, but the audience cannot. Wooning also faces the canvas as he watches Han work. They glance at each other during their conversation, but much of the time they both speak while facing the painting, and thus the audience. Han sometimes contemplates the work, at other times paints quickly and assuredly. Wooning alternately regards the painter and the painting, looking for anything that will show him the truth of things. Projections of various paintings of Han's are visible to the audience. Han's sheer pleasure in creating the forgery is immense and palpable, but he is also desperate to convince Wooning, who remains wary and inscrutable)

HAN. So, you see, I paint over this old canvas, and the crackle is still visible.

WOONING. The old picture underneath is visible?

HAN. No, I scrape away the picture. Not the crackle itself, which is in the original ground layer. I'm careful to preserve that.

WOONING. And what you are painting now...

HAN. Another religious subject. When they are religious, even forgeries make one feel spiritually uplifted. I am, after all, doing God's work. I'm just using a pseudonym.

WOONING. And this one?

HAN. "Young Christ Teaching in the Temple." I painted it myself in 1918. I was in a religious phase, you see. Unlike Vermeer, I actually *had* seen the Italians.

WOONING. You were religious at the time?

HAN. I was an ambitious, womanizing, experimenting art student. I was grateful to God for wine, women and museums, but I never went to church.

WOONING. Perhaps a museum can be a kind of church.

HAN. You're a surprising fellow, Wooning.

WOONING. And you're a dishonest one, if you're telling the truth. So you're doing this subject because you've done it before?

HAN. This particular image, yes. But I would always find a religious story because Bredius is convinced that the secular Vermeer had early in his career been absorbed in religious subjects.

WOONING. And you think that's nonsense.

HAN. It doesn't matter what *I* think. I was only concerned with what Bredius would believe.

WOONING. And you can create an artwork of depth and value without knowing if you believe what you're painting? *(Han stops for a moment and stares at Wooning, who gazes impassively back at him. Han then continues to work.)*

HAN. In addition to the fake crackle, there is the challenge of creating the illusion that the canvas contains the dust of three centuries. So I cover the entire varnished surface — see? — with a layer of India ink.

WOONING. And that's supposed to make me believe you faked all those paintings?

HAN. When it dries, and I remove both the varnish and the ink with turpentine, some of the ink will have penetrated into the crevices in the paint. It will remain there to provide an almost perfect illusion of dust.

WOONING. You're trying to convince me that ink is dust?

HAN. No. But it does look like it. At a casual glance.

WOONING. A casual glance.

HAN. But of course, there would never have been any ink in a painting by Vermeer. So had they ever examined it carefully…

WOONING. They were deciding whether it was great art worth millions. How could they *not* have examined it carefully?

HAN. Because they preferred to believe the illusion was true even when all the evidence indicated the contrary. Have you ever run across that in *your* job?

WOONING. Yes. It's a disease for which there seems to be no cure.

HAN. All that beautiful craftsmanship, and none of it was even necessary to fool them. Look there, at "Woman Reading Music," one of the trial fakes I made before I undertook the "Emmaus." *("Woman Reading Music" is projected so that the audience, as well as Wooning, can see it)* One of my better forgeries, wouldn't you agree? I used seven layers of paint. Seven!

WOONING. But you never sold this one?

HAN. I never intended to. I was perfecting technique to fool Bredius with the "Emmaus."

WOONING. But later. After all the other fakes. Couldn't you have sold this for rather a large sum?

HAN. Perhaps. But it might have been risky.

WOONING. More than the others?

HAN. Oh, yes. This one actually *looks* like Vermeer. It would have been easier to spot as a forgery. I wasn't trying to *copy* Vermeer, remember. I was trying to make them believe I *was* him.

WOONING. You really enjoy this, don't you?

HAN. Don't you enjoy *your* work?

WOONING. I love it.

HAN. With a passion?

WOONING. Yes.

HAN. And it makes you happy?

WOONING. It leaves me satisfied. Sometimes.

HAN. Sometimes. Yes. But I don't paint because it makes me happy. It doesn't. I paint because to *not* paint makes me miserable.

WOONING. And it *was* profitable for you.

HAN. Quite.

WOONING. And when asked about your sudden wealth, you said you'd won the lottery.

HAN. Yes.

WOONING. It would have been relatively easy for someone to discover that you hadn't.

HAN. It would have been easy for someone to have checked for a second layer of paint, let alone a seventh. But no one did.

WOONING. With all that time and the money available, could you not have come up with a more convincing account of your sudden riches?

HAN. Yes. But I didn't need to, did I?

WOONING. *(beat)* You seem to have been somewhat profligate in your spending.

HAN. With each Vermeergeren, it takes half a year at least before the authentication and the sale brings me the money. I find that the more I make, the more I spend in advance, so the more I need by the time I don't need any more.

WOONING. So as you continued to prosper, you took less care with the details of your forgeries?

HAN. Not the signature. I always took the greatest care with his signature.

WOONING. Why?

HAN. Well. It is his, isn't it? *(Han continues to work, and Wooning to watch him, as the lights fade to black and the scene ends)*

Act II
Scene Four

(A month after the previous scene. The Police station. Wooning is interrogating a seated Jo.)

JO. Am I being charged with a crime?

WOONING. *Should* you be?

JO. I suppose that depends upon the crime.

WOONING. Treason is a capital offense. We need to know if you were involved.

JO. I did nothing treasonous, and neither did Han. Do you believe me?

WOONING. I don't know. You're an actress. You're accustomed to pretense.

JO. I'm also accustomed to seeking the truth.

WOONING. Amazing, isn't it? So many of us seeking the truth, so few of us finding it.

JO. May I ask you a question, Inspector?

WOONING. Of course.

JO. When you arrested Han, you said Goering paid highly for "The Adulteress." May I ask how much?

WOONING. One million six hundred and fifty thousand guilders.

JO. That's utter lunacy.

WOONING. I won't disagree with you.

JO. It's a mediocre painting, no matter who painted it.

WOONING. Goering did not pay cash.

JO. How did he pay?

WOONING. He paid in kind.

JO. How do you mean?

WOONING. He returned more than two hundred paintings the Nazis had stolen from The Netherlands. I'm told that many of them are quite valuable, and that their total worth is even greater than the price he agreed to pay.

JO. Are you telling me that Han traded a fake Vermeer to the Nazis for a couple of hundred truly important paintings that have now been returned to our country?

WOONING. That is exactly what I am telling you.

JO. And you're trying him for treason? You should give him a parade! He's a national hero!

WOONING. The two of you did profit handsomely from the sale of the returned paintings. And if he did not know "The Adulteress" was fake…

Jo. Of course he knew! He painted it!

Wooning. So he says. He also says you were completely unaware of his illegal activities.

Jo. You doubt him?

Wooning. Of course I doubt him. He's either a traitor or a fraud. Neither is conducive to my having much confidence in his veracity.

Jo. I have confidence in his veracity.

Wooning. You were his wife.

Jo. That's one reason *why* I was his wife.

Wooning. It is difficult to comprehend how he could have been painting forgeries every day for years without your being aware of them.

Jo. The world is overflowing with things of which I am unaware.

Wooning. And I. But I seek out their explanations.

Jo. I don't.

Wooning. You knew he was painting?

Jo. How could I not?

Wooning. He showed you the work on occasion?

Jo. On occasion.

Wooning. What did you think when you saw it?

Jo. I thought some of it was exceptional.

Wooning. Then you knew what he was doing.

Jo. I knew he was painting.

Wooning. Forgeries.

Jo. Of course not. Why would I think that?

Wooning. Because they were clearly not Vermeer's work. Your husband was standing there painting them.

Jo. They were clearly not Vermeer's work because they don't even *resemble* Vermeer's work. Why would I even *think* of the Master of Delft when I watched my husband painting work not particularly similar to his?

WOONING. What did you think your husband was painting, if not forgeries of Jan Vermeer?

JO. His own work, of course. It's his custom to paint his own work. I've never known him not to. Are you familiar with Han's work?

WOONING. I'm no expert.

JO. How refreshing to hear those words from a man. In that case, Inspector, I truly would value your opinion. Do you find these forgeries similar to the Vermeers you know?

WOONING. I cannot say. I do not know the Vermeers I know. But he was presenting these fakes as genuine.

JO. Have you looked carefully at the faces in Han's forgeries? All his people have the same hooded eyes. He did eyes that way in his own work, as well. Vermeer never did. Examine these paintings, and you'll see for yourself. The same faces with the same hooded eyes, over and over. Yet Bredius and the others never noticed. Ironic, isn't it?

WOONING. In what way?

JO. Figures barely glancing, blinding critics unable to see.

WOONING. Explain something to me.

JO. If I can.

WOONING. You loved your husband.

JO. Yes.

WOONING. You love art.

JO. Great art, always. Good art, sometimes.

WOONING. Integrity is important to you.

JO. As it is to you, Inspector.

WOONING. Yes. Integrity in art and in life.

JO. I don't see the difference.

WOONING. Neither do I. So my question is this: knowing what you now know about Han's work, do you still respect your former husband? Can you still love him?

JO. *(pause)* Is that question relevant to your investigation?

WOONING. It's relevant to me.

JO. *(beat)* I see.

WOONING. You left your first husband for Han.

JO. Yes.

WOONING. Did you know then about van Meegeren's penchant for fakery and fraud?

JO. I knew then that he was a gifted artist who needed to create in his work as I needed to create in mine. I knew he made me feel like the sexiest woman in the world, but he also craved my intelligence as much as he did my flesh. And I knew that life in his presence thrilled me, whereas life without him left me restless and yearning.

WOONING. And that's why you married him?

JO. No. That's why I became his lover. I married him because he made me laugh.

WOONING. And did Bredius make you laugh? *(beat)* You had a relationship with him at one time, did you not?

JO. I still do.

WOONING. An intimate one.

JO. That depends on how you define intimate.

WOONING. It does, doesn't it?

JO. Abraham is homosexual, Inspector.

WOONING. I know. But I make no assumptions.

JO. Impressive.

WOONING. What is?

JO. You seem to have an unusually open mind.

WOONING. That's the only way for anything to enter it, don't you think?

JO. Abraham and I were incompatible. I don't just mean sex. Even if he had been... more inclined that way, I would still have left him for Han, just as I left my husband for Han. I would have left anyone for Han. Han was too much like me for me to not be with him. And Han wanted a partner. Bredius wanted an audience.

WOONING. I'm still unclear how much you understood about van Meegeren when you married him.

JO. I'm not sure I ever really understood my former husband, Inspector. I only know that I risked loving him.

WOONING. Yet he preferred to risk prison. Though he did manage to keep you out of it.

JO. So Han *is* going to prison, and I'm not? Is that what you're saying?

WOONING. I'm not saying anything.

JO. Is that what you're *not* saying?

WOONING. It's difficult to see how he can avoid a prison sentence.

JO. That's a conditional answer.

WOONING. Ours is a conditional existence. Everything in life is a kind of condition, don't you think?

JO. Except love.

WOONING. Not art as well?

JO. Love does not require authentication to those who recognize its worth.

WOONING. And what is its worth, would you say?

JO. Do you know why love is priceless? Because it only achieves its full value when you give it away.

WOONING. But art seems to have its price.

JO. You need to remember, Inspector, that Han only painted the canvases and sold them. He never forced any of these fools to say that the work was Vermeer's. They did that of their own free will. I don't understand why you can't see this from Han's point of view.

WOONING. I do see it. I simply don't like what I see.

JO. Inspector. Have you ever found yourself frustrated by inferior superiors who interfered with your investigations out of envy, incompetence, incomprehension or idiocy?

WOONING. I'm afraid you'll find me unmoved by flattery.

JO. It's not flattery. It's empathy. It's how I feel in my own profession. It's what Han went through every day in his. He saw the earth as round and was crucified by so-called experts who insisted it was flat. How can you condemn him for wanting to expose them for what they are?

WOONING. But he didn't expose them.

JO. Yes, he did. He simply didn't announce it.

WOONING. I admire you deeply, Mrs. van Meegeren. For any number of reasons. But your former husband is either a traitor or a fraud. The only question is which.

JO. Inspector. I get the impression that you have already reached your conclusions. Is that so?

WOONING. Yes.

JO. Then I ask you what they are. I will know shortly in any event. I would consider it a personal kindness if you would simply tell me now.

WOONING. You will not be charged with any crime. I cannot say your responses have convinced me of your innocence, but they have persuaded me that any complicity on your part in your husband's crimes would be impossible to clearly establish.

JO. And Han? Now that you've watched him paint that Vermeergeren for you, do you believe that Han forged those paintings?

WOONING. Yes.

JO. All of them?

WOONING. Yes.

JO. And will that be the conclusion in your official report?

WOONING. Yes.

JO. So Han will not be charged with treason?

WOONING. No. He will be charged with fraud.

JO. The experts are the real frauds.

WOONING. No, the experts are the *other* frauds. *(beat)* Thank you for your assistance in this affair, Mrs. van Meegeren. I am unlikely to ever forget you.

JO. Nor I you. You may not agree, Inspector, but you and Han are essentially alike.

WOONING. We could not possibly be more different.

JO. You both only care about the truth. He in his art, you in your detection. The difference is, he lost his way. I don't imagine that will happen to you. At least I hope not.

WOONING. So do I. And how he lost his way with a wife like you, I cannot comprehend.

JO. Perhaps he lost his way *because* he had a wife like me. *(rises)* Am I free to go?

WOONING. Yes.

JO. Just think, Inspector. If there were more men like you in the art world, none of this need ever have happened.

WOONING. Some mysteries cannot be solved. What makes a work of art great is one of them. I would never be able to reach the truth about that particular question.

JO. No. But you would know you could not. *(He bows to her. She nods and exits as the lights fade and the scene ends)*

ACT II
Scene Five

(A prison cell. 1947. Han sits at a table. Bredius enters. Han rises and bows mockingly)

HAN. After all those months of investigation, then the trial itself, and the verdict afterward, *now* you come to see me?

BREDIUS. They allowed me this one visit.

HAN. Are you here to celebrate the tenth anniversary of your authentication of the "Emmaus?" Or have you come to gloat about my prison sentence?

BREDIUS. What is there to gloat about? You made buffoons of us all. Especially me.

HAN. I couldn't have done it without your help.

BREDIUS. One year's imprisonment. That's all they gave you for such outrageous deceit. The minimum sentence.

HAN. I suppose they were afraid it would be an even greater disgrace to have a trial in which all the art experts were forced to testify at length about why they spent all those millions on work that was only… well… mine.

BREDIUS. A single year's incarceration.

HAN. Weren't the headlines spectacular? "Artist paints for his life!" In the national polls, I am currently the second most popular man in the nation, behind only the Prime Minister. Do you think I should run for office?

BREDIUS. You should be reviled, not celebrated.

HAN. Bredius. Wonderful as it is to see you humiliated — it almost makes the prison sentence worthwhile — surely you're not here to discuss the legal system. How much did you bribe the guard to be alone with me, by the way? I'm always interested in my current market value.

BREDIUS. Why did you sign them?

HAN. What?

BREDIUS. Vermeer left many of his paintings unsigned. If you hadn't signed those fakes with his exact signature, no one would have ever have been able to convict you of forgery. You could have said we chose to authenticate paintings you merely found. You yourself never claimed they were Vermeers.

HAN. My opinion would have been considered worthless.

BREDIUS. It would have *been* worthless. You're just an artist. You don't know anything *about* art.

HAN. At least that was the general assumption.

BREDIUS. Then why? Why not protect yourself?

HAN. I guess I wasn't thinking about protecting myself. I was thinking about tricking you.

BREDIUS. But didn't you always consider me a fool?

HAN. Of course. You *are* one.

BREDIUS. Then why go to such extraordinary effort to prove it, if you were already convinced?

HAN. To make sure that everyone else knew.

BREDIUS. But you ensured instead that no one did. *(beat)* Why did you sign his name?

HAN. I don't really know. *(beat)* Did you notice anything about the signature?

BREDIUS. I noticed everything about the signature. It was flawless.

HAN. Thank you. I can't tell you how much it means to me to hear you say that. But it was also the way Vermeer signed his later paintings. "The I.V. Meer." With the "I" above the middle of the "M" to form the "V."

BREDIUS. Yes, of course.

HAN. Yet if these paintings were authentic, they would have been his *earlier* work. When his signature was different. Didn't that occur to you?

BREDIUS. Of course it did. What do you take me for? Never mind, don't answer that.

HAN. Then how did you reconcile the apparent contradiction?

BREDIUS. I assumed he was trying out the signature that became his later famous one.

HAN. But if he preferred it, which he obviously did, why wouldn't he have kept it once he found it?

BREDIUS. How would *I* know? Look, it was perfect.

HAN. Perfect, but misplaced. Out of context. Tell me: can something be perfect if it doesn't belong where it is?

BREDIUS. I will never understand you, van Meegeren.

HAN. At last, we are in complete agreement about something.

BREDIUS. Why did you lie about the "Emmaus"? When you confessed your forgeries, why insist on including a true masterpiece?

HAN. It's as fake as any of the others.

BREDIUS. We both know you could never have painted anything so glorious.

HAN. I'm unsure whether to be flattered or insulted.

BREDIUS. You're going to insist that it's fake?

HAN. You're going to insist that it's genuine?

BREDIUS. Of course.

HAN. I gave Wooning all sorts of proofs I did it. Told him where to find the missing pieces of wood and canvas. Showed him trial fakes I made first. He believes me.

BREDIUS. That's because he knows nothing.

HAN. Yes, that does seem to have its advantages.

BREDIUS. You will never convince me that "The Christ at Emmaus" is not the work of Jan Vermeer of Delft.

HAN. I've confessed to forging it, proven my guilt to the police, and the whole world is buzzing about my triumph over the clown show that is the art world. Yet you still do not believe I did it?

BREDIUS. My mind, heart, and instincts — my very soul — all tell me that the "Emmaus" is the work of a master.

HAN. Well…

BREDIUS. A real one.

HAN. Ah. Yes. Real. *(beat)* Yesterday, it was worth millions. People from all over the world paid to see it. Today, it is worth nothing and no one would cross the street to see it for free. But the picture itself has not changed. It's either a masterpiece or it isn't, regardless of who created it. Isn't that true? *(They regard each other for a moment, then Bredius shakes his head in wonder)*

BREDIUS. If that pretentious Nazi who thinks he knows great art had not bought your fake, we would all have gone to our graves thinking your forgeries were real. No one would have ever known.

HAN. The papers say Goering learned I tricked him while he awaits trial at Nuremberg. An eyewitness said he looked as if for the first time, he had discovered there was evil in the world.

BREDIUS. You went to all that trouble, for what? For money?

HAN. No. Money only became important later.

BREDIUS. Then you went to all that trouble for nothing.

HAN. It wasn't for nothing! And it wasn't just for the money, or the fun of it, or simply to destroy your reputation, though I did enjoy all of those. I also wanted to show you the work of which I was capable, the genius you refused to acknowledge in me, even as your predecessors denied it to Vermeer. God, you don't recognize it even now! You attribute my most successful work to someone else!

BREDIUS. Your legacy is that you will be remembered as a forger of Vermeer. Tell me, do you think anyone will ever be known as a forger of van Meegeren?

HAN. I am an artist. You are not. People like you, who admire achievements you can never accomplish, always try to destroy those like me, living reminders of a gift you can only envy. God gave me my talent. Who are you to judge it?

BREDIUS. Vermeer dreamed of a future in which his artistry would finally be revered. You dream of a day when your fakery will finally be acknowledged. You don't see the difference? *(Bredius starts to depart. Han comes to a sudden decision, rises and addresses him)*

HAN. Bredius. Wait. I will show you the truth.

BREDIUS. I cannot imagine anyone less qualified to do so. *(turns to go)*

HAN. *(intense)* Just... describe the painting. *(Bredius stops and faces him)*

BREDIUS. What do you mean?

HAN. "The Supper at Emmaus." Describe what you see in the picture. Not the skill or technique. Just the event. The story itself.

BREDIUS. What in God's name...

HAN. Please. It's the last thing I'll ever ask of you. Just tell me the story of the painting.

BREDIUS. This is ridiculous. *(He turns to go, but Han's urgent voice stops him)*

HAN. Cleopas and his friend have been traveling with a stranger, and they sit down to supper with him. They suspect nothing; he is just another wanderer. Then...

BREDIUS. *(beat)* Then he lifts the bread, and they recognize him as the Christ.

HAN. Luke — the only gospel that tells this story — says: "as he sat at meat with them, he took bread, and blessed it, and brake, and gave it to them. And their eyes were opened and they knew him; and he vanished out of their sight."

BREDIUS. What's your point?

HAN. You saw the moment of recognition in the painting?

BREDIUS. Of course I saw it.

HAN. Tell me what you saw. Please.

BREDIUS. Christ has raised his hand to bless the bread.

HAN. *(eagerly)* And Cleopas is stunned?

BREDIUS. Overcome with awe. The other man's face is of course not visible in Vermeer's rendering.

HAN. But, you see... that was Caravaggio.

BREDIUS. What was?

HAN. The moment of recognition. Christ reveals himself by raising his hand. Cleopas realizes who he is. That's what Caravaggio painted. In both of his versions.

BREDIUS. As Vermeer did in this one.

HAN. No. You've looked, but you have not seen.

BREDIUS. Seen what?

HAN. I painted the moment just *before* recognition. Christ has just begun to raise his hand, but he has not yet revealed himself. Cleopas and his friend show no understanding at all. They will, but only in the moment *after* this one. When they will finally see their Savior clearly, only to have him instantly vanish before their uncomprehending eyes.

BREDIUS. You are quite mistaken.

HAN. They were doubters, you see. They did not recognize the Son of God even as he sat right next to them. I wanted to capture their ignorance for eternity.

BREDIUS. I don't see…

HAN. No, you don't. *(beat)* Those two critics will sit in that painting, at that table, waiting for a piece of bread, oblivious to their redeemer, for the rest of time. That is how I preserved them for posterity. They will remain forever unaware of the divinity in their midst. Eternally unenlightened. They will never know. They will never be saved. *That* is what you do not see. *(There is a pause as the two men regard each other, taking each other's measure. Then Bredius speaks)*

BREDIUS. But you never blessed the bread, did you? You just baked and ate it. Without a grace. *(beat)* You didn't really destroy my reputation, you know. You only damaged it a bit. The next time I authenticate a painting, everyone will accept my word for it just as they always did before. *(beat)* After all, who else is there to tell them what is real, and what is not? *(He leaves. Han sits there. The lights fade on him and rise on a projection of the "Emmaus" as the play ends)*

END OF PLAY

Pronunciations

Meegeren	MAY-ger-en.
Bredius	BRAY-dee-us
Wooning	VOH-ning
Theo van Wijngaarden	TAY-o van VAYNE-yarden
de Hooch	de HOEck
de Groot	de GROet
Emmaus	Em-MAY-us

Costumes, Set Pieces and Props

- **ACT I SCENE ONE:** An art gallery, Rotterdam, 1936

Costumes:
Bredius — Distinguished suit
Jo — impeccably tasteful dress for a gallery's opening night

Set pieces and props:
projections of paintings

- **ACT I SCENE TWO:** A bedroom, Rotterdam, still 1936

Costumes:
Han — bedclothes
Jo — nightgown

Set pieces and props:
a bed   paintings   easels   a magnifying glass

- **ACT I SCENE THREE:** Artist's studio. Rotterdam, still 1936

Costumes:
Han — painter's work garb
Jo — tastefully casual outfit

Set pieces and props:
paintings   paints and accoutrements
easels   a projection of the "Emmaus" painting

- **ACT I SCENE FOUR:** Bredius's living room, Rotterdam, 1937

Costumes:
Bredius — casually elegant, expensive outfit
Jo — tasteful but not too formal dress

Set pieces and props:
two snifters with "brandy"   projection of the "Emmaus" painting

- ACT I SCENE FIVE: A living room. Rotterdam, 1938

Costumes:
Han — casual clothes
Jo — nice but low-key outfit

Set pieces and props:
a book (actually a playscript)   a ring

- ACT I SCENE SIX: An art gallery. Rotterdam, 1938

Costumes:
Bredius — casually elegant, expensive outfit
Han — tasteful but not too formal clothes

Set pieces and props:
projection of the "Emmaus" painting

- ACT I SCENE SEVEN: A living room. Rotterdam, 1943

Costumes:
Han — casual clothes
Jo — professional suit

Set pieces and props:
a dartboard with Hitler's face on it
a number of darts
more lavish surroundings and expensive furniture than was in this room previously

- ACT I SCENE EIGHT: A living room. Rotterdam, 1945

Costumes:
Han — casual clothes
Jo — dinner dress
Wooning — innocuous suit, deliberately nondescript looking

Set pieces and props:
even *more* lavish surroundings and expensive furniture than was in this room previously

- ACT II SCENE ONE: A police station interrogation room. 1945

Costumes:
Wooning — same innocuous suit
Han — same casual clothes from Act I, Scene 7

Set pieces and props:
table   two chairs   lamp

- **ACT II SCENE TWO:** A police station interrogation room. 1945

Costumes:
Wooning — a different innocuous suit
Bredius — formally elegant, expensive outfit

Set pieces and props:
table   two chairs   lamp

- **ACT II SCENE THREE:** An artist's studio. Rotterdam, 1945

Costumes:
Han — old, beat-up, stained painter's working clothes
Wooning — a boring suit

Set pieces and props:
a large canvas (58¾ × 75½) that faces upstage
projections of various paintings of Han's visible to the audience: including "Woman Reading Music" and "Young Christ Teaching at the Temple"

- **ACT II SCENE FOUR:** A police station interrogation room. 1945

Costumes:
Wooning — another innocuous suit
Jo — a subtly sexy dress

Set pieces and props:
table   two chairs   lamp

- **ACT II SCENE FIVE:** A police station interrogation room. 1947

Costumes:
Han — prison garb
Bredius — elegant, expensive outfit

Set pieces and props:
table   two chairs   lamp
a projection of the "Emmaus" painting

About the Playwrights

In 2010, **Hilary Bettis** was named the first recipient of a playwriting fellowship, sponsored by Tony-Award winning actress Cherry Jones and administered by the Abingdon Theatre, to celebrate the career of a female playwright under the age of thirty. Ms. Bettis, a 2010 semifinalist for the Juilliard Lila Acheson Wallace Playwright Fellowship, was already the 2009 recipient of the John N. Wall Fellowship for playwriting at the Sewanee Writer's Conference, and had received two fellowships from New River Dramatists in 2009. Her play *American Girls* was produced Off Broadway at the 45th Street Theatre in 2008, and was anthologized in *Best Monologues of 2009* and *Best Stage Scenes of 2008*, both published by Smith & Kraus. Attack Films produced her first screenplay, *B'Hurst*, as a short film in the summer of 2008, and she is working on a feature-length version. Before Ms. Bettis began writing, she worked as a professional actress in New York and Los Angeles. She is a member of SAG, AEA, the Dramatists Guild, and the Playwrights Center, a lifetime member playwright at the Ensemble Studio Theatre in New York, and an affiliated artist with New Georges.

Wendy Hammond's plays have been produced by several New York City as well as regional theatres. Her plays have also been staged in London, Singapore and Melbourne. In addition to *Absence*, her works include *Julie Johnson, Family Life: 3 Brutal Comedies, Jersey City,* and *The Ghostman*. *The Hole*, produced at the Purple Rose Theatre in 1999, was nominated by the American Theatre Critics Association for best new American play. Her screenplays include *Julie Johnson*, produced by Shooting Gallery Films, co-written by director Bob Gosse, starring Lili Taylor, Courtney Love and Spalding Gray. The film premiered at the Sundance Film Festival in 2001, and played in film festivals all over the world, winning many awards including Best Feature in the Barcelona Film Festival and an Audience Award in Berlin. Ms. Hammond wrote and directed the short film *Lehi's Wife* (in post-production in 2011) through AFI's Directors Workshop for Women. She is a recipient of an NEA grant, an NYFA grant, a McKnight Fellowship and a Drama League Award. Ms. Hammond has been invited twice to the Sundance Play Unit, twice to the O'Neill Center, and several times to New River Dramatists in North Carolina. She is also an alumna of New Dramatists in New York and she holds an MFA from New York University's Dramatic Writing Program and a master of divinity degree from Yale Divinity School. She has taught playwriting and screenwriting courses at several universities, including the University of Michigan and Brown. She is currently on the faculty of NYU's Tisch Asia School of the Arts in Singapore where she lives with her beloved son.

M. Z. Ribalow has had 24 of his plays receive some 180 productions worldwide, including at Dublin's Abbey Theatre, at the Edinburgh Festival, and numerous times in London and New York. They have won awards in London, New York, and regionally. His work has been published, anthologized and filmed. He has also won national awards for his widely published poetry, fiction, and musical lyrics; he has co-written ten children's books and published articles on sports, music, theatre, literature, film, travel, and chess. In addition to the novel *Peanuts and Crackerjacks* (2011) and the poetry collection *Chasing Ghosts* (2011), he is the co-author of three books on sports and the director of an award-winning sports website. Several of his screenplays have been optioned; he was film columnist for *The Sciences* magazine, and has appeared as a film historian on the Discovery Channel and on special feature documentaries of several DVD releases of classic films. He is a co-founder and Artistic Director of New River Dramatists, and hosts New River's radio show at Art On Air online. He was Joseph Papp's production associate at the New York Shakespeare Festival for several years, then founded the American Repertory Company of London, producing two four-play seasons. He was vice-president of the Creative Coalition (of which he was a founder) as well as international arts coordinator of the Global Forum, where he worked with the Dalai Lama, Robert Redford and Mikhail Gorbachev. He is currently a full-time artist-in-residence at Fordham University, and also teaches at the William Esper Studio.

Acknowledgments

Of the many people who have helped make the dream that is New River possible, several have helped in ways that were invaluable and unwavering. We could never have realized our creative haven without Dasha Shenkman, our International Chair, and Gayle Winston, our luminous and incomprehensibly generous host at River House. Wilton and Catherine Connor, John and Edie Crutcher, Robert Franklin, Jerry Heymann, Bud and Zanne Baker, Bruce and Jo Marie Lilly, John and Pam Anderson, Wallace Colvard and Tom Wilson, among others, have tirelessly given not only financial support but generously of their time, talents and unflagging efforts. Bill Baker was for years a one-man staff at New River. Leslie Carroll, in addition to her contributions as an actor, served as our pro bono literary manager and organized all the early work written at our sessions. Randell Haynes and Patricia Randell have both been not only core actors, but also tremendous resources with their extensive knowledge of actors and playwrights. Sam McGregor was always there when we needed her, and Spencer Humphrey provided redoubtable expertise. The late and loved Jim McLure, a participating playwright, was supportive in so many other ways as well, and we will always miss him. And nothing we have done would have been possible without the support and preternatural understanding of Laura Woods.

www.ingramcontent.com/pod-product-compliance
Ingram Content Group UK Ltd.
Pitfield, Milton Keynes, MK11 3LW, UK
UKHW042011140426
5217IPUK00015B/1115